LOVED AND UNASHAMED

A Chapter-by-Chapter Journey through Romans

SAM RAINER

Loved and Unashamed:
A Chapter-by-Chapter Journey through Romans

ISBN 979-8-9954034-0-1

Church Answers
Franklin, Tennessee

Printed in the United States of America

To Erin

My wife, my love

CONTENTS

INTRODUCTION

The Context Behind the Letter

Romans is one of the most important letters ever written. Historically, few books in the Bible have carried the doctrinal weight, spiritual depth, and transformative power of Paul's letter to the Romans. While every one of Paul's letters addresses a particular situation, Romans rises above as the most comprehensive theological explanation of the gospel and its implications. To understand why Romans matters, and why believers across history have returned to it again and again, we must understand the purpose behind the letter.

Paul wrote thirteen New Testament letters, each born out of specific needs within the church. Sometimes he encouraged, as in Philippians. Sometimes he corrected, as in Corinthians. Sometimes he defended the true gospel against false teaching, as in Galatians. Each letter reflects the reality that the early church was growing rapidly across diverse locations, cultures, and challenges. Letters became the preferred method of guiding, shaping, and strengthening these communities of believers scattered across the Roman Empire.

Paul's own story underscores the authority and urgency behind his writing. Once known as Saul—a zealous Pharisee, determined to destroy Christianity—he encountered the risen Jesus on the Damascus Road. That encounter changed everything. His name changed. His calling changed. His allegiance changed. The man who once sought to imprison Christians would become the missionary who planted churches, nurtured their growth, endured persecution, and proclaimed Jesus to Jews and Gentiles alike.

His unique background prepared him for this monumental mission. As a Roman citizen, he could travel freely. With a Greek education, he could speak into the philosophical world of the Gentiles. With a deep Hebrew religious heritage, he carried unmatched knowledge of God's law and covenant history. After his conversion, Paul spent years preparing before embarking on missionary journeys that would reshape the spiritual landscape of the world.

Romans emerges from this missional passion. Unlike some of Paul's other letters, Romans was not written primarily to address a crisis, correct immorality, or rebuke false teachers. Instead, Romans is written to ground the church in truth, unite Jewish and Gentile believers, and present the clearest gospel message in the New Testament.

Romans as the Church's Doctrinal Foundation

The placement of Romans after Acts is intentional and instructive. Acts tells us *what* God did to expand the church. Romans explains *why* He did it and *what it means.* Acts shows movement. Romans provides meaning. Acts demonstrates growth. Romans provides grounding. Romans is the longest of Paul's letters and the deepest theologically. Paul writes not merely to inspire, but to form the bedrock of Christian belief. The purpose of Romans is to help believers understand the gospel clearly, embrace it fully, and live it faithfully.

Paul structures Romans with remarkable intentionality. The first half of the book (chapters 1–8) establishes doctrine. Here, Paul lays out the condition of humanity, the righteousness of God, the necessity of Christ, the role of faith, and the work of the Holy Spirit. He confronts sin honestly. He explains justification masterfully. He unfolds grace beautifully. Romans 1 begins with a sobering diagnosis: humanity is trapped in sin, spiritually dead, helpless, and unable to save itself. But Paul does not leave us in despair. He declares that righteousness comes not through human effort or religious performance, but through faith in Jesus Christ.

In these opening chapters, we encounter core doctrines of the Christian faith:

- Regeneration — God gives new spiritual life to dead sinners.

- Conversion — We respond willingly to the gospel through faith and repentance.
- Justification — God declares us righteous through Christ's sacrifice.
- Adoption — God welcomes us into His family.
- Sanctification — God continually shapes us into Christ's likeness.

Paul's purpose is not simply to define salvation theoretically. He wants believers to marvel at it, cherish it, and rest secure in it. Romans proclaims that Christians are no longer condemned, no longer enslaved, and no longer under the power of sin. In Christ, they live in freedom and assurance.

The Gospel Explained, Defended, and Applied

Romans also uses a powerful rhetorical style called *diatribe*. Through a series of questions and responses, Paul anticipates objections, addresses confusion, and dismantles false conclusions. This method allows Paul not merely to teach doctrine but to shepherd thinking. He guides his readers to see the logical and spiritual implications of truth. For example:

- Should we keep sinning so grace can abound? *Absolutely not.*
- Does grace give permission for lawlessness? *Never.*
- Is the law itself sinful? *Of course not.*

Paul understands that Romans is shaping the theological imagination of the church. He clarifies not only what the gospel is but also what it is not. In doing so, he protects the church from distortions and preserves the purity of faith.

Israel, the Nations, and the Sovereignty of God

Another major purpose of Romans is to explain God's plan for Israel and the Gentiles. In chapters 9–11, Paul wrestles with Israel's unbelief. He acknowledges grief over those who reject Christ but reminds the church that God's promises have not failed. Through Israel, God brought the Messiah. Through Israel's rejection, salvation spread to the Gentiles. God is sovereign. God is faithful. God is at work, weaving redemption through history. This section helps the church understand identity. Gentile believers are not replacing Israel but being grafted into God's redemptive story. Israel's story is not discarded; it is fulfilled in Christ.

Doctrine Leads to Life

After constructing one of the greatest theological explanations ever written, Paul turns practical. Chapters 12–16 answer this question: *If this is what God has done for us, how should we live?*

Romans makes it unmistakably clear—right doctrine produces right living. The gospel does not create passive believers or detached intellectuals. It forms people who love sacrificially, serve humbly, pursue unity, show grace, honor authority rightly, and live as living sacrifices to God.

Paul paints a picture of a gospel-shaped community:

- A people transformed in mind and life.
- A people who love sincerely.
- A people who reject vengeance and embrace forgiveness.
- A people committed to unity in diversity.
- A people who live out their faith in everyday obedience.

Romans is not theoretical theology. It is applied theology. Its purpose is not simply to inform but to form disciples who embody the gospel.

A Letter That Changes Lives

Throughout history, Romans has changed hearts, reshaped the church, and fueled reformations. Augustine surrendered to Christ while reading Romans. Martin Luther found assurance of salvation there and declared Romans the "chief part of the New Testament." Countless believers have encountered grace, certainty, and a sense of calling through its pages.

Why? Because Romans explains the gospel with clarity unmatched anywhere else in Scripture. It reveals who God is, who we are, why we need salvation, how salvation happens, and what redeemed life looks like. It is doctrinally rich, spiritually profound, intellectually engaging, and eternally significant.

The purpose of Romans is to ground the church in the gospel of Jesus Christ, deeply, clearly, and unshakably. It develops doctrine. It strengthens faith. It unites believers. It clarifies the plan of God. It challenges pride. It confronts sin. It elevates grace. And ultimately, it calls us to live as people transformed by the righteousness of Christ.

Romans is not always easy reading, but it is always worth reading. It stretches the mind, convicts the heart, and strengthens the soul. Its purpose is nothing less than to anchor believers in the unchanging gospel and to call the church to live for the glory of God. In Romans, the church receives not merely instruction but identity—people saved by grace, secure in Christ, empowered by the Spirit, adopted by the Father, and sent into the world as living testimonies of the righteousness and mercy of God.

CHAPTER 1

The Gospel That Makes Us Right with God

Romans 1

Romans opens not with casual pleasantries but with purpose and urgency. The Apostle Paul writes to believers in Rome as a man utterly captured by Christ. Once a persecutor of Christians, Paul now identifies himself as a *slave* of Jesus Christ, "chosen" and "sent" to proclaim the Good News. From the very first verse, Paul establishes a foundational reality: Jesus is not our personal assistant; He is our King. To belong to Christ is to live under His authority, for His glory, and in submission to His mission.

Paul's calling clarifies our calling. The opening verses remind believers that we too have been "called by God to be his holy people" (Romans 1:7, NLT). Before Paul ever addresses sin or doctrine, he centers the reader in this profound identity: we are loved by God. And because we are loved, we are also called. Christianity is not merely about forgiveness; it is also about purpose. God sets His people apart to carry His Good News into the world.

Romans is one of the most important letters ever written. Where Acts records the expansion of the early church, Romans develops the doctrine that would shape the church for centuries. It presents a sweeping vision—why the world is broken, what God has done about it, and how believers live in light of His saving work. The letter divides into two broad sections: theology and doctrine in chapters 1–8, and practice and application in chapters 9–16. Paul does not separate belief from behavior. Theology leads to transformation.

The Heartbeat of Romans: Loved and Unashamed

Midway through the opening chapter, Paul names the theme that beats through the entire letter:

> "I am writing to all of you in Rome who are loved by God and are called to be his own holy people." (Romans 1:7, NLT)

> "For I am not ashamed of this Good News about Christ. It is the power of God at work, saving everyone who believes... This Good News tells us how God makes us right in his sight." (Romans 1:16–17, NLT)

These verses are the keystone of Romans. Since you are "loved" by Jesus (1:7), you should be "unashamed" (1:16) to share His Good News. The gospel is not religious advice, self-help inspiration, or moral philosophy. "The gospel is God at work." Salvation is not something we achieve. It is something God accomplishes. From beginning to end, from "start to finish," it is entirely God's doing. Paul writes as a man who has placed his full confidence in this message. He does not hesitate. He does not apologize. He is unashamed. Why? Because he knows who he is in Christ. He knows he is loved by God. And those who know they are loved live unashamed.

We often try to establish our own righteousness, working desperately to be acceptable. But Paul reminds us that righteousness is not a human achievement. It is a divine gift. Righteousness means being "right with God," pleasing in the only eyes that ultimately matter. We are not righteous because of our performance. We are righteous because Christ has made us right through His life, death, and resurrection.

Righteousness is our right standing before God, made possible by His justifying work through salvation in Christ. Left to ourselves, we instinctively try to manufacture that standing. We work to be presentable because we want approval. It's like the difference between a first date and a twenty-fifth date. On the first date, you hide the flaws and present the best version of yourself. You don't order a giant burger at the restaurant because it might give you gas. By the twenty-fifth date, everything is out in the open—Taco Bell and no pretending. Our own standards shift over time, even in relationships, which exposes the fragility of self-made righteousness.

That's the problem with self-righteousness: it never holds, because the standard keeps changing. We might ask whether we are righteous by our own measures, but the real question is whether we are righteous by God's unchanging standard. Unlike ours, His expectations do not fluctuate. This is why we must stop making righteousness about anything other than what Christ has done for us. True righteousness is not about what we have done right, but about being made right through Jesus. Real righteousness is being pleasing in the sight of the only eyes that ultimately matter—God's.

A Gospel of Power

Paul emphasizes that the gospel *saves.* It does not merely inspire spiritual sentiment. It does not offer theoretical improvement. It rescues. God saves real sinners in a real world through the real work of Jesus Christ. He saves Jews and Gentiles, the educated and uneducated, the civilized and the uncivilized. The gospel is for everyone. Faith is not belief in an abstract idea. Faith is trust in a living Savior. The message of Jesus Christ is active and powerful. When we proclaim Christ crucified and risen, God works. When we place our faith in Him, God justifies. When we surrender to Him, God transforms.

The Tension of Love and Wrath

But immediately after declaring the glory of the gospel, Paul confronts the human condition. "God shows his anger from heaven against all sinful, wicked people who suppress the truth by their wickedness" (Romans 1:18, NLT). Here, Paul addresses a reality modern culture resists: God's wrath.

Yet Paul insists that wrath and love are not opposites. They belong together. Perfect love cannot be indifferent toward evil. A parent who watches a child self-destruct and feels nothing cannot be loving. True love opposes whatever destroys the beloved. In this way, God's wrath is not divine cruelty; it is a holy, protective, and righteous love. God's anger toward sin exists because He is deeply committed to the flourishing of those He loves.

And here is the staggering truth. Only God's love can satisfy God's wrath. What God demands, God Himself provides. Jesus bore the full weight of divine wrath on the cross. He stood in our place, absorbing judgment so that those who believe would be freed forever from condemnation. For believers, there is no wrath left. None. Christ has taken it all.

The Human Problem: The Downward Spiral of Sin

Romans 1 gives us one of Scripture's clearest portraits of what happens when humanity rejects God. Paul writes that God's truth is plain. His existence and power are visible in creation. Yet people ignore Him. Rather than worshiping the Creator, they worship creation. Rather than embracing truth, they exchange it for lies. Rather than honoring God, they exalt themselves.

Paul describes a downward spiral:

- They ignore the truth.
- They worship creation instead of the Creator.
- They believe Satan's lies.
- They act in degrading ways.
- They refuse God's grace.
- They confuse others, leading them deeper into sin.

This downgrade is not merely an ancient description. It is a diagnosis of the human condition. When a society removes God from the center, something else always fills the space—power, pleasure, politics, identity, or self-worship. Sin does not simply appear; it progresses. Hearts harden. Minds distort. Lives unravel. And the results are devastating: wickedness, greed, hatred, envy, violence, deception, sexual brokenness, rebellion, cruelty, and relational destruction.

Paul's point is not that *they* are sinners, but that *we all* are. In the very next chapter, he warns, "You may think you can condemn such people, but you are just as bad" (Romans 2:1, NLT). No one escapes guilt. Everyone stands in need of grace. The problem is universal, and therefore the gospel must be universal as well.

But Romans 1 is not a passage of despair. It is a passage of honesty that prepares us for hope. Paul shows us the depth of our sin so that we might grasp the fullness of God's provision. The spiral of sin is real, but it is not final. There is a way out. Jesus saves. Where shame enslaves, the gospel frees. Where sin destroys, grace restores. Where wrath condemns, mercy rescues. God does not abandon humanity to its rebellion. He pursues. He redeems. He restores.

Living Loved and Unashamed

Romans 1 is not simply about doctrine; it is about identity. Paul reminds believers in Rome—and us—that we are "loved by God and called to be his holy people" (Romans 1:7, NLT). This identity frames the Christian life. Because we are loved, we do not live in fear. Because we are accepted, we do not strive for approval. Because we are justified, we do not carry shame. The gospel forms a people who are loved and unashamed.

To be unashamed does not mean arrogant. It does not mean combative. It means confident in Christ. It means anchored in truth. It means bold in witness. It means refusing to hide our faith or silence our hope because the gospel is too powerful, too beautiful, and too necessary to keep to ourselves. In a world drowning in guilt and confusion, Christians carry the message of freedom and clarity. In a culture that chases lies, believers hold the truth. In a society filled with shame, the church proclaims grace. Paul writes Romans so that the church will be strong, clear, holy, joyful, and mission-driven.

Romans 1 lays the foundation for the entire letter. It confronts us with who God is: holy, loving, powerful, and sovereign. It confronts us with who we are—sinners desperately in need of grace. And it confronts us with who we can become—people made right with God, freed from wrath, rescued from sin, and sent into the world with Good News. The gospel is not passive. God is at work. He is saving. He is calling. He is forming a people who live loved and unashamed. That is the promise of Romans. That is the invitation of chapter one. And that is the journey that unfolds through the rest of this remarkable letter.

Chapter 1 Reflection Questions
The Gospel That Makes Us Right with God

1. What does it mean to be "loved by God," and how does that identity shape the way we live?
2. Why is Paul so confident and unashamed of the gospel, and what might keep believers today from sharing it boldly?
3. How does Romans 1 reveal both the seriousness of sin and the depth of God's love?
4. In what ways does our culture "exchange the truth for a lie," and how can believers stand firm in truth?
5. How does understanding the power of the gospel change the way you view your salvation and your mission?

CHAPTER 2

Why We All Need Christ's Righteousness

Romans 2

The first chapter of Romans exposes the obvious darkness of the world: idolatry and open rejection of God. It is easy to read that chapter and nod in agreement. Yes, the world is broken. Yes, sin is real. Yes, people are running from God. But Paul does not allow us to remain spectators, shaking our heads at "those people." Romans 2 turns the spotlight, not outward, but inward. It confronts not only the rebellious but also the religious. It reveals why every person desperately needs the righteousness of Christ.

The key confession of the chapter is this: righteousness is not about what we have done right. It is about being made right through Jesus. Paul's concern in Romans 2 is not primarily with scandalous sinners but with self-assured saints—people who believe their morality, heritage, or religious knowledge places them in good standing before God.

God's Standard and God's Impartiality

Romans 2 opens with a devastating reality check:

> "You may think you can condemn such people, but you are just as bad, and you have no excuse!" (Romans 2:1, NLT)

The point is unmistakable. The same people who condemn the sins of others commit sins of their own. We are quick to see rebellion in others and remarkably slow to recognize hypocrisy in ourselves. Paul exposes the double standard at the heart of self-righteousness. We judge others by their actions and ourselves by our intentions. Then Paul states the principle that demolishes all spiritual superiority:

> "For God does not show favoritism." (Romans 2:11, NLT)

God does not grade on a curve. He does not have different expectations for different people. Every person stands before the same holy God under the same righteous standard. Jewish or Gentile, moral or immoral, religious or irreligious—every human being will be judged with perfect justice. This truth is both humbling and hopeful. It humbles those who assume God prefers them because of their heritage, traditions, or knowledge.

It gives hope to those who fear they are beyond God's concern. God's impartiality means no one is automatically accepted and no one is automatically excluded. All are sinners. All need grace. All may come to Christ.

The Law and the Illusion of Moral Superiority

Paul next addresses a critical misunderstanding in the religious mind: the assumption that knowing God's law equals obeying it. He writes,

> "For merely listening to the law doesn't make us right with God. It is obeying the law that makes us right in his sight." (Romans 2:13, NLT)

The Jewish people had been given the law at Mount Sinai. They possessed Scripture. They knew commandments, rituals, and traditions. The Gentiles, Paul says, have the work of the law written on their hearts. Their consciences bearing witness to moral truth. Whether written on tablets of stone or impressed upon the conscience, God's standard is known. And still no one keeps it perfectly. That is Paul's argument. Knowledge cannot save us. Identity cannot save us. Being part of the right group, holding the right book, or quoting the right verse cannot save us. The law reveals God's will and exposes human failure, but it cannot rescue us from that failure.

Paul's image of the law is deeply pastoral. He reminds us that God's law is not a cruel restriction but a loving safeguard. It protects us from "the tyranny of our own sin" and guides us into life-giving obedience. God's commands are not shackles but safety. They are like the fence around a yard bordered by busy highways, not a barrier to joy, but a boundary for life.

Yet even this gracious law is twisted by self-righteous hearts. Instead of submitting to God under the law, religious people often use the law to justify themselves and condemn others. They clutch truth without practicing it. They possess knowledge without humility. They mistake information for transformation.

When Religion Becomes a Mask

Romans 2 exposes the tragedy of religious pretense. Some of Paul's Jewish readers believed they enjoyed a "special relationship" with God that made them superior to others. They were convinced they were "guides for the blind," "lights for those in darkness," and "teachers of children" (see Romans 2:17–20). Their assumption was clear: We know the law, so we are right with God.

Paul disagrees. He points out that their failure to obey the law they so confidently taught actually dishonored God and turned others away. He quotes the sobering indictment,

> "The Gentiles blaspheme the name of God because of you." (Romans 2:24, NLT)

Hypocrisy is not a victimless sin. It wounds the church. It repels unbelievers. It distorts the name of Christ. When those who claim to follow God publicly betray His truth, the watching world is not merely disappointed; they are disillusioned. Paul's message is timeless. Church affiliation, moral reputation, or theological vocabulary cannot substitute for obedience. You can love the Bible without reading it, quote Scripture without understanding it, and defend truth publicly while disregarding it privately. God is not fooled. People may judge the façade. God judges the heart.

Two Streams of Righteousness

Paul introduces a crucial distinction: two competing visions of righteousness. One is *form righteousness*—shaped by rules, rituals, identity, and obligation. It is self-centered, obsessed with appearances, and rooted in pride. It confuses external markers with internal reality. The other is *heart righteousness*—shaped by grace, truth, sacrifice, and mission. It is Christ-centered, empowered by the Spirit, and rooted in surrender.

Paul uses circumcision as an example. For Jews, circumcision marked covenant identity. But Paul insists outward ceremony without inward transformation is meaningless. True covenant identity is not physical but spiritual, not a mark on the body but a change of heart accomplished by the Holy Spirit (Romans 2:28–29).

This reality raises the chapter's essential question: What makes a person righteous? Paul answers by stripping away every false foundation:

- Not heritage.
- Not knowledge.
- Not morality.
- Not religious practice.
- Not good intentions.

Righteousness is relational, not performative. It is "the fulfillment of expectations within a relationship," being made right with God through Christ's work, not ours. We do not achieve righteousness. We receive it.

The Danger of Self-Righteousness

Paul warns that self-righteousness is not merely misguided; it is spiritually deadly. It blinds us to our sin, hardens us against repentance, and despises God's kindness. He describes the warning signs:

- You overestimate your goodness.
- You underestimate your depravity.
- You do not recognize God's holiness.

The result is tragic. Instead of allowing God's patience to lead to repentance, the self-righteous "store up" wrath for themselves

(Romans 2:5). Grace, meant to melt the heart, is treated instead as permission to remain unchanged. That is why Romans 2 is so searchingly honest. It calls us to stop pretending and to abandon the exhausting charade of image management and moral comparison. Self-righteousness says, "Accept me for who I pretend to be." The gospel invites us into the freedom of being fully known and fully forgiven.

The God Who Knows Our Secrets

Marriage has a way of pulling hidden things into the light. Living closely with another person exposes the habits and quirks you didn't even realize you had, or maybe hoped no one would notice. Years ago, my wife, Erin, caught me in one of those secret bad habits. I was standing in her parents' kitchen, casually drinking straight from the milk jug like a teenager who had forgotten basic manners. She saw it. Judgment was swiftly issued. Wrath followed. Repentance came just as quickly—and to this day, I've never done it again. It's one of those small sins we can laugh about now, the kind that becomes a running joke in marriage.

But not every hidden sin is funny. Most secrets aren't quirky flaws. They're embarrassing, damaging, and deeply consequential. The truth is, we all carry things we'd rather no one see: thoughts, choices, and failures we hope stay buried. Yet nothing is hidden from God. He knows every secret in your life, all of them. Not just the harmless ones, but the heavy ones too. Marriage may expose a few habits, but God sees the whole heart. And that reality humbles us, reminding us that we don't stand before Him based on what we hide, but on the grace He gives.

Perhaps the most sobering line in Romans 2 is this:

> "The day is coming when God, through Christ Jesus, will judge everyone's secret life." (Romans 2:16, NLT)

Nothing is hidden from God. Not our thoughts. Not our motives. Not the habits we excuse, conceal, or justify. Everything we manage carefully before people is already fully known before God. For the self-righteous person, this is terrifying. For the repentant person, it is liberating. God does not expose to humiliate, but to heal. He reveals to redeem. The judgment of secrets does not merely condemn; it drives us to Christ, the only One whose righteousness can cover our guilt.

Why We All Need Christ's Righteousness

Romans 2 crushes the illusion that good people go to heaven because of their goodness. Paul will later say clearly, "No one is righteous—not even one" (Romans 3:10, NLT). Romans 2 is the bridge into that conclusion. Pagans fall short. Moralists fall short. Religious leaders fall short. Everyone falls short. The remedy is not self-improvement or stricter obedience. The solution is Christ. We need a righteousness we cannot produce. We need a record we cannot earn. We need a Savior we do not deserve.

That is why Paul's call is so powerful: stop pretending. Stop relying on your moral resume. Stop hiding behind religious performance. Stop trusting in your goodness. Start trusting in Christ. When we do, something glorious happens. Righteousness moves from *form* to *heart*, from *rule keeping* to *Spirit transformation*, from *external conformity* to *internal renewal*. The Holy Spirit circumcises the heart. Desire changes. Identity changes. Direction changes. Life changes.

Living Loved and Unashamed

Romans 2 prepares us for the good news yet to come in Romans 3–5. It levels the ground at the foot of the cross. There are no insiders and outsiders based on performance. We are all sinners. We are all loved. We are all invited. The call of Romans 2 is not merely to behave better; it is to believe rightly. To abandon self-righteousness and rest in Christ's righteousness. To walk in honest repentance rather than polished hypocrisy. To live loved and unashamed.

God knows your secrets. God sees your heart. God offers you Christ. And Christ is enough. In the end, Romans 2 is not a call to despair over sin but to delight in grace. It reveals the emptiness of moral pride so we can experience the fullness of gospel joy. It tells the truth about us so we can rest in the truth about Jesus. So come out from behind the façade. Lay down the mask of self-righteousness. Stop pretending and start living in the freedom, honesty, and power of Christ's righteousness.

Chapter 2 Reflection Questions
Why We All Need Christ's Righteousness

1. Why is self-righteousness so spiritually dangerous, even for sincere religious people?
2. How does God's impartiality humble the proud and give hope to the broken?
3. What is the difference between "knowing" God's truth and "living" God's truth?
4. How can religious activity become a substitute for genuine obedience?
5. Why must righteousness come from Christ rather than human effort?

CHAPTER 3

The Verdict That Changes Everything

Romans 3

Imagine a courtroom. The evidence is overwhelming. The defendant stands silent because there is no defense left to offer. The judge is just, the law is clear, and the sentence is certain. Paul constructs this image in Romans 3. Humanity is not merely flawed. We are guilty. We have not simply made mistakes—we have broken God's law. And judgment is not a distant hypothetical reality; it is the spiritual condition of every person apart from Christ.

Romans 3 is one of the clearest explanations of the human problem and God's answer. If Romans 1 revealed the universal reach of sin and Romans 2 stripped away the illusion of self-righteousness, then Romans 3 delivers the verdict: *no one is righteous.*

Not one. As Paul writes, "For no one can ever be made right with God by doing what the law commands. The law simply shows us how sinful we are" (Romans 3:20, NLT). We are guilty, and we cannot defend ourselves. We cannot justify ourselves. And yet, this chapter is also where the brightest hope breaks through. God does what we cannot. He justifies sinners through Jesus Christ.

The Universal Problem: We Are Not Righteous

The heart of Romans 3 begins with a sweeping declaration:

> "No one is righteous—not even one." (Romans 3:10, NLT)

That sentence levels humanity. There is no category of people exempt from this reality. Paul dismantles every argument that someone might present in their own defense. Jew or Gentile. Religious or secular. Educated or uneducated. Moral or immoral. No one meets God's standard. No one fulfills His expectations. No one can stand before Him and claim innocence. We are all guilty.

Paul wants us to feel the weight of this truth. It is not meant to crush hope but to reveal reality. Until we understand the depth of our sin, we will never understand the magnitude of grace. If we believe we are mostly good, we will see Jesus as a helpful addition rather than an absolute necessity. But when we understand our true spiritual condition, we recognize that without divine intervention, there is only condemnation. Paul summarizes the problem using courtroom language. God is the Judge. We are the accused. We have broken the law. The verdict is guilty. Judgment is deserved. And judgment is certain.

One of the greatest misunderstandings people carry is the idea that religious effort or moral obedience can rescue them. But Paul crushes that false hope:

> "For no one can ever be made right with God by doing what the law commands." (Romans 3:20, NLT)

The law of God was never meant to save us. It was meant to expose us. Consider the image of an X-ray. An X-ray reveals a fracture, but it cannot mend it. It diagnoses without curing. It uncovers damage without providing healing. That is exactly what God's law does. It reveals how sinful we are. So the question arises: if the law exposes guilt and we cannot justify ourselves, is there any hope?

The Breakthrough of Grace: Justification

To "justify" something in everyday life means to argue that what you did or said was reasonable and right. We do it all the time, particularly in conflict. Think about an argument with your spouse. It often turns into a back-and-forth exchange of self-defense, with each person insisting, "I'm the one who's right," while the other says the exact same thing. But if we can't even win those debates at home, what makes us think we could ever win one with God? Do we really believe we can stand before Him and explain away all our actions as reasonable and righteous? Justification reminds us that we don't prove ourselves right before God. He declares us right through His grace.

Romans 3 contains one of the most glorious turning points in all of Scripture:

> "Yet God, in his grace, freely makes us right in his sight. He did this through Christ Jesus when he freed us from the penalty for our sins." (Romans 3:24, NLT)

Here, Paul introduces the doctrine of justification. If righteousness is fulfilling God's expectations, justification is God's legal declaration that we are forgiven, accepted, and declared right in His sight. We are not *made* righteous because we suddenly become morally perfect. Instead, we are *declared* righteous because Christ has taken our guilt and given us His righteousness.

Justification is a courtroom term. It is the opposite of condemnation. To be condemned is to be declared guilty and sentenced. To be justified is to be declared innocent and freed. And Romans 3 announces that justification is not something we earn. It is something God gives. Freely. Graciously. Paul explains how this salvation works:

- The Holy Spirit convicts us of sin.
- God begins regenerating our hearts.

- We respond to Jesus through repentance and faith.
- God converts us and welcomes us into His family.
- God justifies us, freeing us from sin's penalty.
- The Holy Spirit sanctifies us throughout life.
- God glorifies us when we enter His presence.

Salvation is wholly God's work, but we must respond in faith. We cannot work our way to God. We cannot argue our way to innocence. We cannot justify ourselves. Only God can declare us righteous, and He does so through Jesus Christ.

The Judge Who Became the Substitute

Romans 3 places us in the courtroom. The Judge sits on the bench. Humanity stands condemned. Justice demands judgment. But here is where the gospel becomes breathtaking. Jesus is the Judge. Jesus is the One against whom every sin is ultimately committed. Jesus is the rightful authority. And yet, Jesus does what no earthly judge could ever do. He steps down from the bench, removes the robe of justice, and stands in the place of the guilty. He does not dismiss justice. He satisfies it. He does not ignore sin. He bears it. He takes our penalty upon Himself.

Paul explains that we are "made right with God when [we] believe that Jesus sacrificed his life, shedding his blood" (Romans 3:25, NLT). The punishment we deserved for sin was placed fully upon Him. Isaiah prophesied this reality centuries earlier:

> "The Lord laid on him the sins of us all." (Isaiah 53:6, NLT)

Jesus becomes our substitution. The innocent stands in place of the guilty. The holy suffers for the unholy. The righteous takes the punishment of the unrighteous. Jesus was condemned so that we could be justified. The Judge became the Savior. The verdict over our lives changes from "guilty" to "declared righteous."

If justification is truly God's work, then there is no room for pride. Paul says we have "nothing to boast about" because we did nothing to earn salvation. We did not behave our way to acceptance. We did not impress God into forgiving us. Our acquittal is not based on obedience to the law but on faith in Christ. Grace is received, not achieved. God does not save the morally polished. He saves sinners who trust Jesus. And it is available to everyone. Romans 3:22 states:

> "We are made right with God by placing our faith in Jesus Christ. And this is true for everyone who believes, no matter who we are." (NLT)

That means no past disqualifies you. No failure removes you from grace's reach. No background limits God's invitation. Paul began this chapter addressing Jewish concerns. What advantage was there to being entrusted with God's Word if everyone is still found sinful? Paul's answer is that God's faithfulness shines all the more. Even when people are unfaithful, God remains perfectly true. His promises do not fail. His righteousness is unwavering.

Romans 3 also clarifies an uncomfortable but necessary truth: judgment is real. Jesus will judge everyone. John 3:18 declares that those who do not believe remain under judgment already. Judgment is not simply a future possibility; it is a present condition for those apart from Christ. But Romans 3 also tells us how to escape that judgment—by believing in Jesus.

Some people struggle with the idea of God as Judge. But without a Judge, there is no justice. Without judgment, evil goes unanswered. Without divine justice, there is only despair. A world without judgment is a world where oppression has no consequence, where wickedness has no accounting, where suffering has no resolution. Judgment is not a problem. It is a promise. God will make all things right. But there is a deeper beauty. The Judge we fear is the Judge who loves us. The Judge we face is the Judge who stepped into our place. We do not simply have a Judge; we have a Savior-Judge who ensures both justice and mercy. That is why Romans 3 is not a chapter of despair. It is a chapter of breathtaking hope.

The Verdict That Changes Everything

Romans 3 leaves us with no illusions about ourselves and no confusion about grace. We are guilty. We cannot justify ourselves. The law exposes our sin but cannot heal us. We stand condemned in the courtroom of heaven. But God, in His grace, freely declares us right in His sight through Jesus Christ. Justification is not symbolic. It is not partial. It is not probationary. It is final. Absolute. Eternal. When God declares a sinner righteous through Christ, heaven's verdict is forever sealed.

Past sins are forgiven. Christ's righteousness is credited to us. We are adopted into God's family. We walk not in shame but in grace. We live not in fear but in assurance. This is why believers can live loved and unashamed. Not because we are flawless, but because Christ is faithful. Not because we are righteous, but because we are clothed in His righteousness. Romans 3 calls us to stop trying to justify ourselves. To stop pretending we can stand in court on our own merit. To stop believing we can earn God's approval. Instead, we are invited to trust Jesus completely, rest in His finished work, and rejoice in a verdict that changes everything. The Judge has spoken. The sentence has been paid. The guilty have been declared righteous. And through Jesus Christ, we are free.

Chapter 3 Reflection Questions
The Verdict That Changes Everything

1. Why is it important for believers to understand the reality of human guilt before God?
2. What does justification mean, and why is it central to the Christian faith?
3. How does grace remove all boasting from the Christian life?
4. Why is Jesus' substitution in our place such a powerful truth?
5. How does the verdict of "declared righteous" provide assurance and peace for believers?

CHAPTER 4

Father Abraham and the Family of God

Romans 4

Romans 2 taught us that righteousness is fulfilling God's expectations. Romans 3 revealed that none of us can meet those expectations on our own, but that God justifies us through Christ. Now, in Romans 4, Paul takes us backward before he takes us forward. He reaches deep into the Old Testament to show that this has always been God's way. Salvation has never been earned. It has always been given. Righteousness has never been achieved through effort. It has always been received through faith.

Paul anchors his argument in the story of Abraham, the man Israel rightly esteemed as the father of their nation. If anyone might have had a spiritual "advantage," surely it was Abraham—the patriarch, the covenant bearer, the first man through whom God began building a people. But Romans 4 asks a critical question: How did Abraham become right with God? Was it by his works? His obedience? His heritage? Or was it something else entirely?

Paul answers emphatically: Abraham was "counted as righteous" because of his faith. Before the law. Before rituals. Before religious markers. Abraham trusted God, and God credited righteousness to him. Faith—not performance—brought Abraham into right standing with God. And that truth changes everything, not just for Israel, but for the entire world.

When the Law Can't Save You

Paul begins Romans 4 by reminding us that the law, while good and holy, cannot rescue us. In fact, he says, "The law always brings punishment on those who try to obey it" (Romans 4:15, NLT). That statement is not a condemnation of God's law but of our inability to keep it. The more we try to use obedience as our lifeline, the more we are confronted with how far short we fall. The law reveals sin, exposes guilt, and shows us just how desperately we need grace.

That's why the story of the woman caught in adultery in John 8 is such a powerful illustration. She was undeniably guilty. The Pharisees seized her sin as an opportunity to trap Jesus—forcing Him, they believed, to choose between compassion and conviction. Jesus is placed in what seems like an impossible dilemma: care for the woman or uphold the Law. If He sides with the Law, they can accuse Him of lacking compassion. If He sides with the woman, they can claim He rejects God's commands. They expect Him to choose between grace and judgment. Instead, Jesus does neither and both. He never declares her "not guilty," because she is guilty. But He also doesn't condemn her. In essence, He says, "Guilty. Forgiven. Now stop it." Grace does not deny sin but rather offers a remedy for it.

That is what Paul is teaching in Romans 4. The law cannot forgive. Sin must be dealt with. Wrath is real. But what the law cannot do, Jesus does. Through faith in Him, we receive justification, a full and final declaration of forgiveness and acceptance before God.

Paul brings King David into the conversation as well, quoting Psalm 32:

> "Oh, what joy for those whose disobedience is forgiven, whose sins are put out of sight.
> Yes, what joy for those whose record the Lord has cleared of sin."
> (Romans 4:7–8, NLT)

David knew sin. He knew the crushing weight of moral failure. And he also knew the liberating power of forgiveness. Paul highlights David because he represents something essential: the happiest people in God's kingdom are not the most impressive. They are the most forgiven. "The most joyful people in the world are the most repentant," because the joy of grace can only be experienced when sin is honestly confessed and truly forgiven.

That's why Romans 4 presses us toward a right view of sin and grace. Some take too high a view of themselves: "I don't need forgiveness." Some take too low a view: "I'm beyond forgiveness." The gospel rejects both. True faith says, "I am forgiven because of Christ." It is not my goodness that saves me. It is not my failure that disqualifies me. It is Jesus alone.

Abraham and the Covenant of Grace

To understand why Abraham matters so deeply, we must remember his story. In Genesis 12, God calls Abraham out of his homeland—not with a map but with a promise. Abraham obeys. God tells him that his descendants will become a great nation, that land will be given, and that through Abraham "all the families of the earth will be blessed."

Israel was chosen not because the nation was superior, more moral, or more loved than others. They were chosen as the family through whom grace would extend to the world. The Old Testament tells the story of God revealing His redemptive plan primarily through Israel. God made covenants—an eternal covenant with Noah, an everlasting covenant with Abraham, a royal covenant with David, and the promise of a new covenant through Jeremiah. That new covenant is fulfilled in Jesus. He does not abolish the old covenant; He completes it. Through His death and resurrection, the promise to Abraham finally becomes accessible to everyone who believes.

Paul asks another important question in Romans 4: Who receives the blessing promised to Abraham? Is it limited to those who share his ethnicity, his rituals, or his law? Or does it extend further? Paul answers: The blessing belongs to those who share Abraham's faith. Abraham was counted righteous before circumcision, before the formal sign of covenant identity. This timing matters. It proves righteousness did not come through ritual. It did not come through ceremony. It did not come through national belonging. It came through faith. Therefore, Abraham becomes the "father" of all who believe. He is the prototype of salvation, not by works, but by trust in God's promise.

Paul writes beautifully, "People are counted as righteous, not because of their work, but because of their faith in God who forgives sinners" (Romans 4:5, NLT). And again, "So the promise is received by faith. It is given as a free gift... For Abraham is the father of all who believe" (Romans 4:16, NLT). This is not simply theology. It is identity. The true family of God is not built through heritage, ritual, or moral accomplishment. It is built through faith. If you trust Christ, you stand in the same lineage of faith as Abraham. You belong to God's covenant family.

Grace, Not Karma

Paul's discussion naturally raises a question: if salvation comes by faith, why do so many insist on treating it like a performance system? Why do people instinctively believe they can earn God's love or secure His approval through effort? Romans 4 pushes us to confront the difference between grace and every other religious instinct. Grace means getting from God what you do not deserve. Karma—ironically embraced in many secular ways of thinking—means getting exactly what you deserve. Karma collapses under the weight of real suffering. Karma does nothing in the face of tragedy. Karma cannot comfort a grieving parent, sustain a soldier, or heal a terminal diagnosis.

We need something better. We need grace. Grace is unmerited favor from an unobligated Giver. We don't deserve it. God does not owe it. Yet He freely gives it. Grace exists because we are totally incapable of saving ourselves. Self-improvement has its place, but it cannot resurrect the spiritually dead. Trying to work your way to salvation is like shouting louder at a lifeless body, hoping it will rise. It cannot. Only God gives life. Only grace saves. That is why Scripture repeatedly insists: salvation is not by works. Ephesians 2:8–9 proclaims that salvation is by grace through faith, not ourselves, not our merit, not our resume, so that no one can boast.

Faith: The Only Right Response

Romans 4 closes with gospel clarity. Abraham's story is not an isolated Old Testament episode. It is a blueprint. Abraham shows that salvation has always been "by grace alone, through faith alone, in Christ alone." Those in the Old Testament trusted the promise God made that would ultimately be fulfilled in Christ. We trust the promise, now fulfilled in Christ and openly declared to us.

Paul makes sure we understand that Romans 4 is not just about ancient figures. It is about us. Christ died "to forgive our sins" and rose "to prove redemption true." His resurrection secures the promise. His grace is available to every repentant, believing heart today. And when grace is received, it transforms. Like the woman in John 8, grace does not dismiss sin. It overcomes it. Grace forgives. Grace restores. Grace calls us to new life. Grace says: "Neither do I condemn you." Grace also says, "Now go and live like someone who has been changed."

Romans 4 is not merely a theological defense. It is a declaration of belonging. Through faith in Christ, you are part of something ancient and eternal. You stand in the same family as Abraham. You share in the covenant promises of God. You don't enter by heritage. You don't hold your place by performance. You remain not because of your strength but because of His grace. And that is exhilarating. God owes us nothing, yet gives us everything. Those forgiven most deeply rejoice most fully. Those who trust Christ most completely live most freely. Those who belong to God's family live loved and unashamed. Abraham believed God. David trusted God. Every believer since has placed their hope in God the Son, Jesus. And so do we. The promise still stands. The invitation still extends. The family of faith is still open. By grace. Through faith. In Christ alone.

Chapter 4 Reflection Questions
Father Abraham and the Family of God

1. What does Abraham teach us about faith and righteousness?
2. Why is salvation always a matter of grace rather than works—even in the Old Testament?
3. How does belonging to the "family of faith" shape our identity as believers?
4. What does true repentance and forgiveness produce in the life of a believer?
5. How does understanding grace protect us from both pride and despair?

CHAPTER 5

Unlocking the Goodness of God

Romans 5

Locks exist because something precious must be protected. We lock our homes to guard what matters inside. We lock our devices to protect our identities. To access something locked, you need the right key. Romans 5 opens with a stunning reality. There are treasures in the Christian life that cannot be accessed through morality or religious activity. They are locked behind a door that can be opened only with one key. Paul tells us what that key is: Faith in Jesus Christ.

Paul writes, "Because of our faith, Christ has brought us into this place of undeserved privilege where we now stand, and we confidently and joyfully look forward to sharing God's glory"

(Romans 5:2, NLT). Faith ushers us into something we could never earn: grace. Faith opens the door to what God freely gives: peace, hope, confidence, endurance, reconciliation, and life.

Romans 5 answers an important question: What does justification produce in the life of a believer? If chapters 2–4 explain righteousness and justification, chapter 5 reveals the blessings they unlock. Grace is not merely a theological category. It is a living reality that reshapes who we are, how we live, and how we endure.

Peace That Sends Us Into the World

Paul's first declaration is breathtaking:

> "Since we have been made right in God's sight by faith, we have peace with God because of what Jesus Christ our Lord has done for us." (Romans 5:1, NLT)

Justification gives us peace *with* God. The war between heaven and our rebellious hearts is over. The hostility produced by sin has been resolved. God does not tolerate us. He reconciles us. But Romans 5 does not describe peace as an escape from sorrow. God's peace does not remove us from hard places. It calls us into them. Jesus promised peace in John 14:27—peace unlike anything the world can offer. It is not the absence of trouble. It is the absence of fear. Jesus, the "Man of Sorrows," knew suffering intimately but was never governed by fear. In the same way, those who possess God's peace are not paralyzed by hardship but strengthened to walk faithfully through it. God's peace sends us into the world's sorrow with courage, compassion, and purpose.

Paul even insists that believers will "run into problems and trials" (Romans 5:3, NLT). Following Christ does not insulate us from pain. But pain is no longer meaningless. Suffering becomes a forge for spiritual growth. Paul outlines a chain reaction of grace: suffering produces endurance; endurance produces character; character produces hope. Hope is not fragile optimism. Paul describes hope as the convergence of confidence and security. It is rooted in the unchanging love of God and the indwelling presence of the Holy Spirit. "And this hope will not lead to disappointment," Paul writes, "for we know how dearly God loves us" (Romans 5:5, NLT). Hope in Christ never collapses. It sustains. It steadies. It assures. Through faith, we stand in "undeserved privilege" before God as secure and confident people.

Faith That Holds Us Secure

Romans 5 does not merely tell us God loves us. It proves that He does. Paul confronts us with the most astonishing statement in the chapter:

> "But God showed his great love for us by sending Christ to die for us while we were still sinners." (Romans 5:8, NLT)

Rarely would anyone die for another person. Perhaps someone might die for a good person (Romans 5:7), but Christ died for His enemies. Paul emphasizes we were "utterly helpless" when Christ died for us (Romans 5:6, NLT). We had nothing to offer. No moral leverage. No spiritual credit. No righteousness of our own. Yet Jesus came "at just the right time." He did not wait for us to improve. He did not wait for us to get serious, spiritual, or strong. He loved us at our worst and gave us His best. Through Christ's death, Paul says we are "certainly saved from God's condemnation" (Romans 5:9, NLT). Through Christ, we are no longer enemies of God but friends. We are restored to Him. Redemption is not theoretical. It is relational restoration, complete acceptance, secure belonging.

Hebrews 11:1 says faith is the evidence of what we cannot see. Faith anchors us in God's promises, not in our performance. Romans 5 is emphatic: faith brings us into grace, and grace keeps us secure. Christian faith is not a blind leap into uncertainty. It is confident trust in the character of God. Faith is not weak sentiment. It is active confidence. If you have faith, you believe. If you believe, you trust continually. Faith placed in God, fueled by God, sustained by God, leads to victory. But perhaps the most profound section of Romans 5 begins in verse 12, where Paul widens the lens from personal faith to the sweeping narrative of redemption history.

Adam and Christ: The Story of Two Men

Paul contrasts two figures who define humanity—Adam and Christ. Adam represents the origin of sin and death. Through his disobedience, sin entered the world. With sin came death. Humanity inherited not only Adam's nature but also Adam's guilt. This reality explains why the world is broken, why hearts are rebellious, and why suffering feels universal. Even before the formal giving of the law, people were sinning and dying. Paul makes the stunning point that God had not yet "invoiced" the full legal charges for sin between Adam and Moses, but death still reigned because sin was present. In other words, humanity had accumulated a debt it could never pay.

Then Paul introduces a theological reality essential to Christian faith—imputation. To "impute" is to transfer something to another's account. In Romans 5, Paul explains:

- Adam's guilt is imputed to us — resulting in condemnation.
- Our sin is imputed to Christ — because of the atonement.
- Christ's righteousness is imputed to us — resulting in justification.

This process is the miracle of grace. We owed God a debt beyond repayment. Jesus takes the invoice and pays it fully with His blood. Paul summarizes this in breathtaking contrast:

- "Adam's one sin brings condemnation for everyone" (Romans 5:18, NLT).
- "Even greater is God's wonderful grace" (Romans 5:15, NLT).

One man broke the world. The other man saved it. Adam's disobedience unleashed ruin. Christ's obedience restores life. Adam leads humanity away from God. Jesus leads us back to God.

Grace That Rules

Romans 5 answers another deeply important question: If sin is so pervasive and powerful, what hope is there? Paul's answer is emphatic: grace is stronger. He explains why the Old Testament and the law still matter. The law did not create sin; it revealed it. It showed humanity how sinful we truly are. But as sin increased, grace increased all the more. "God's wonderful grace became more abundant," Paul writes (Romans 5:20, NLT). Scripture gives an honestly bleak portrait of human failure. The Old Testament ends with longing. When will redemption come? When will God deliver? Why is the world still broken? Romans 5 gives the answer:

> "Just as sin ruled over all people and brought them to death, now God's wonderful grace rules instead... resulting in eternal life through Jesus Christ our Lord." (Romans 5:21, NLT)

Sin once ruled. Death once reigned. Despair once dominated. But now—grace rules. Grace outruns sin. Grace overwhelms guilt. Grace overturns condemnation. Grace overpowers death.

Unlocking the Goodness of God

Romans 5 is not merely a chapter about doctrine; it is a declaration of life. It tells us what faith unlocks:

- Peace with God.
- Access to grace.
- Hope that does not fail.
- Endurance in suffering.
- Love proven beyond doubt.
- Salvation from wrath.
- Friendship with God.
- New identity in Christ.
- Victory over death.
- Eternal life under the reign of grace.

Paul asks in effect: How do you unlock God's goodness? His answer is simple and glorious: *Grace is the key. Faith is the hand that turns it.* You do not receive God's goodness by performance. You do not earn His favor by improvement. You cannot secure His approval by moral effort. You open your hands, surrender your pride, confess your helplessness, and trust Jesus. Romans 5 stands as a triumphant declaration that believers live under a new kingdom—where peace replaces hostility, hope replaces despair, love replaces shame, and grace rules forever. And because grace rules, believers live loved and unashamed.

Chapter 5 Reflection Questions
Unlocking the Goodness of God

1. What blessings become ours when we are justified by faith?
2. How does peace with God transform the way we see suffering and hardship?
3. Why is God's love demonstrated most clearly at the cross?
4. What does it mean that grace now "reigns" in the believer's life?
5. How does hope in Christ anchor us when life feels uncertain?

CHAPTER 6

How Sin's Power is Broken

Romans 6

Romans 6 confronts one of the most universal fears known to humanity—the fear of death—and proclaims one of the Bible's most liberating truths: in Christ, the power of sin is broken and the dominion of death is defeated. Romans 1–3 reveals our guilt. Romans 4 shows how we are justified by faith. Romans 5 celebrates the goodness of God's grace. But Romans 6 answers the critical question: *If grace saves us, how do we live now?* Paul's answer is both theological and deeply practical. Grace does not excuse sin; grace liberates us from its control. Sin's penalty is dealt with through justification, and now sin's power is broken through union with Christ.

The Fear We Cannot Escape on Our Own

Fear affects everyone. Some fears fade. Others linger. Some are reasonable. Others are irrational. But there is one fear humanity rarely escapes—the fear of death. Why? Because death feels final. It represents the unknown. It exposes our inability to control our destiny. It reminds us we are mortal.

Romans 6 explains why death feels so heavy: "The wages of sin is death" (Romans 6:23, NLT). Death exists because sin exists. Death is not merely a biological event; it is a spiritual and eternal reality.

Scripture teaches that death has three dimensions. There is ***physical death***, the separation of body from spirit. There is ***spiritual death***, the separation of the soul from God in this life. And there is *eternal death*, the final judgment and separation from God for those who reject Christ. Sin is the poisonous root beneath every death experience. "For sin is the sting that results in death" (1 Corinthians 15:56). We die because we sin, and as long as sin rules us, death reigns over us.

But Romans 6 doesn't leave us in despair. It proclaims the gospel's triumphant answer: through Christ, death dies. When Jesus went to the cross, He absorbed sin's penalty. When He rose from the grave, He destroyed death's authority. "When he died, he died once to break the power of sin... so you also should consider yourselves to be dead to the power of sin and alive to God through Christ Jesus" (Romans 6:10–11, NLT). Through Christ, death no longer has the last word. Through Christ, we no longer live enslaved to fear. God even calls the death of His people "precious" (Psalm 116:15). What once symbolized doom now serves as the doorway into eternal life for believers. There is no need to fear what has been conquered.

Romans 6 teaches that something miraculous happens at salvation: believers are united with Christ. We are united with Him in His death, meaning the old self is crucified. Our sin was nailed to the cross with Jesus. But we are also united with Him in His resurrection, meaning we are made alive to God. Our identity changes. Our spiritual condition changes. Our destiny changes. Paul says believers "live new lives" through the power of God. The Christian life is not moral self-improvement. It is resurrection life. Sin's *penalty* has been addressed through justification. Now sin's *power* is shattered through union with Christ. Death fulfills the demand of sin, but death also opens the pathway to resurrection life. This means something profoundly practical: Christians do not need to fear death because life now comes *through* it. And Christians do not need to live controlled by sin because its authority has been broken. Sanctification begins.

Sanctification: Living Free with the Holy Spirit

Paul shifts the conversation from salvation to spiritual formation. Salvation makes us legally righteous. Sanctification makes us increasingly holy. Romans 6 introduces sanctification as the lifelong process in which believers cooperate with the Holy Spirit to grow in holiness, obedience, and Christlikeness. When Jesus saves you, God expects you to live for Him and like Him. Sanctification requires intentional participation. While all believers are equally justified, not all believers are equally sanctified because not all believers cooperate equally with the Spirit's work. That is why Paul urges:

> "Do not let sin control the way you live... give yourselves completely to God."
> (Romans 6:12–13, NLT)

Grace is never an excuse to sin. Grace is the power to stop sinning. Paul revisits the question he first raised earlier in Romans—if grace increases when sin increases, should we just sin more? "Of course not!" he declares. "We are no longer slaves to sin." To continue living in deliberate rebellion after salvation is to misunderstand grace entirely. John Knox captures Paul's thought perfectly: "How can we who have died to sin breathe its air again?" Sin may tempt us, but it no longer owns us. We are free. Justification is what Christ does for you. Sanctification is what you do with the Holy Spirit. God has broken sin's chains. Now we are to walk in freedom.

Freedom Misunderstood

Romans 6 introduces one of Paul's most powerful metaphors—slavery. He acknowledges the weight of the comparison, but he uses it purposefully. Every person serves something. Everyone has a master. "You are a slave to whatever you choose to obey" (Romans 6:16, NLT). Modern culture treats freedom as the ability to do whatever we want. Scripture treats freedom as the ability to live as God designed. Christianity clarifies something our world resists—total permissiveness and total oppression are both forms of slavery.

In *permissive* cultures, Christianity seems restrictive—too narrow, too limiting. In *oppressive* cultures, Christianity seems dangerously liberating—too free, too threatening. Paul's point is striking: neither legalism nor license brings freedom. Legalism binds you in fear and religious exhaustion. License promises self-freedom but ends in self-destruction. True freedom is found only in Christ. He is the only Master who liberates, the only Lord who gives life, the only authority who heals instead of enslaving. What you live for will rule you. Your purpose will become your master. Live for money, and you become its slave. Live for pleasure, and it consumes you. Live for approval, and you become imprisoned by opinions. Live for self, and you will eventually destroy yourself. Live for Christ—and you will finally be free.

That is why Paul says believers become "slaves of God," not because God oppresses, but because surrendering to Him is the only path to holiness, wholeness, and joy. When you submit to Christ, you are set free to become who God created you to be. Freedom is not found in resisting God. Freedom is found in belonging to Him.

Freedom Obtained

Romans 6 reaches one of the most familiar and powerful statements in Scripture:

> "For the wages of sin is death, but the free gift of God is eternal life through Christ Jesus our Lord." (Romans 6:23, NLT)

Sin pays out exactly what it promises—death. But God offers something sin never can: eternal life. Not earned. Not deserved. Not negotiated. A gift. Free. Available to all who trust in Christ. Through His cross, sin's penalty is satisfied. Through His resurrection, death is conquered. Through His Spirit, believers are empowered to live in newness of life. God does not only save you *from* something. He saves you *for* something: holiness, purpose, peace, and eternal life.

Romans 6 confronts us with two crucial questions. First: do you belong to Christ? If not, sin still rules, and death still reigns. But if you trust Jesus, the verdict changes forever. Sin loses authority. Death loses power. Fear loses ground. Grace reigns. Second: if you are a believer, are you cooperating with the Holy Spirit? Freedom from sin does not mean believers never struggle. It means we never again have to surrender. Sanctification is the daily act of choosing obedience, resisting sin, yielding the body and will to God, and walking in newness of life.

Romans 6 delivers a life-giving message. Death does not own you. Sin does not define you. Fear does not control you. Christ has broken the chains. Christ has conquered the grave. Christ has given you freedom. Now live like someone who is truly alive. In Christ, sin's power is broken. Death is defeated. Fear is silenced. And believers are free. Truly free.

Chapter 6 Reflection Questions
How Sin's Power Is Broken

1. How does union with Christ change our relationship to sin?
2. Why is grace not permission to sin but power to resist it?
3. What does it practically mean to "present ourselves" to God?
4. How does understanding slavery to sin help us appreciate true freedom in Christ?
5. Why is sanctification a cooperative process with the Holy Spirit?

CHAPTER 7

Winning the War with Your Mind

Romans 7

Have you ever settled something deep in your soul—what you know is right, what you know God wants—only to have your mind refuse to cooperate? You lie awake replaying options, arguments, doubts, and temptations. Your heart wants obedience. Your soul longs for God. But your mind feels like a battlefield you keep losing. Paul knew that struggle. He lived that tension. And in Romans 7, he describes it with raw honesty.

Romans 7 is one of the most emotionally vulnerable passages Paul ever wrote. It is startling in its candor. If Romans 6 declares sin's power is broken, Romans 7 admits sin's presence still feels overwhelming. If Romans 5 shouts victory, Romans 7 whispers frustration. This is the tension every believer feels. Saved, but still battling. Forgiven, but still tempted. Rescued, but still wrestling. Paul describes it this way:

> "I want to do what is right, but I can't. I want to do what is good, but I don't. I don't want to do what is wrong, but I do it anyway." (Romans 7:18-19, NLT)

There is a war within. Paul confesses, "There is another power within me that is at war with my mind" (Romans 7:23, NLT). He wants righteousness. He desires obedience. He genuinely loves God and His law. But something inside refuses to cooperate. As most of us know, this struggle is not theoretical theology. It is a lived reality. Romans 7 makes something clear: following Jesus does not remove the battle; it reveals it and gives us the tools to fight for victory.

Before Paul describes the war within, he explains how believers relate to the law. Using the analogy of marriage, he says that just as a woman is bound to her husband until death, so we were once bound to the law. But a death has occurred. Christ died. Because of His death, we died to the power of the law. Now, through His resurrection, we are united to Him instead. We no longer serve God under fear-based duty, but in the life-giving freedom of the Spirit (Romans 7:1–6).

Paul is clear: the law was not evil. The law revealed God's holiness. But the law could not make us holy. It revealed sin; it could not remove sin. It exposed guilt; it could not erase guilt.

That is why grace was necessary. The law points us to Christ; Christ frees us from the condemnation of the law. But freedom from condemnation does not automatically mean freedom from struggle. That is the reality Paul now confronts.

Why Don't I Do Good?

Paul voices the question every believer eventually asks: Why don't I do good when I want to? Why do I do what I hate? Why do I keep falling? Why do I think thoughts I shouldn't think? Why does temptation feel so loud? In verse 14, Paul identifies the problem: "The trouble is with me, for I am all too human, a slave to sin." Sin has roots still active in our flesh. Though sin's penalty is broken, its influence lingers. We live with divided desires—the redeemed self longing to obey God and the sinful flesh resisting.

Scholars debate whether Paul is describing his life before Christ or his ongoing Christian experience. He writes in the present tense. His words sound like an ongoing struggle rather than a distant memory. Perhaps the ambiguity is purposeful. Paul may be giving voice to the human condition in general: the capacity for failure before salvation, and the ongoing tension even after salvation. Either way, the message is clear. Apart from Christ, we lose this war.

The Battle for the Mind

Paul's battle is not only behavioral. It is mental. He says explicitly, "There is another power within me that is at war with my mind." That is not a poetic description. It is a diagnosis. Your mind is not neutral territory. It is contested ground. What occupies your thoughts directs your life. Jesus commanded us to love God with heart, soul, and *mind* (Matthew 22:37). Scripture distinguishes but intertwines these elements of who we are:

- *Heart*: the seat of our desires and affections.
- *Soul*: the whole essence of who we are, our identity, and life.
- *Mind*: our reasoning, thinking, and discerning capacity.

The heart is like the steering wheel. It directs where we want to go. The soul is like the engine. It is the life force of movement. The mind is like the dashboard. It interprets reality, warns, measures, and informs direction. All three must submit to God. But our culture tells us the opposite. We are told to follow our hearts, prioritize emotions, and elevate feelings above truth. The great cultural lie is: *Your feelings define you. Your emotions are your truest guide.*

Paul calls us to something far different. He reminds us later in Romans, "Let God transform you into a new person by changing the way you think" (Romans 12:2, NLT). Transformation happens through renewed thinking. Truth forms godliness. Right thinking fuels right living. Your feelings cannot be your moral compass. They fluctuate. They mislead. They are easily influenced. But the renewed mind anchors us to God's will.

Satan does not need to destroy you to defeat you. He only needs to confuse your thinking.

He only needs to convince you to trust your desires more than God's truth. This is why Paul's struggle feels so modern. His tension is ours. His fight is ours. His war is ours. And his honesty gives every believer permission to say, "Yes, even saved people struggle." *Even faithful Christians wrestle. Even the most devoted saints battle sinful thoughts, impulses, and weakness.*

Who Will Rescue Me?

Romans 7 moves toward one of the most desperate and beautiful cries in Scripture:

> "Oh, what a miserable person I am! Who will free me from this life that is dominated by sin and death?" (Romans 7:24, NLT)

That cry matters. It is the confession of someone who has reached the end of self-sufficiency. As long as we believe we can outthink sin, overpower temptation, and out-discipline our flesh, we will continue losing. Victory comes only when we confess defeat apart from Christ. The answer comes immediately:

> "Thank God! The answer is in Jesus Christ our Lord." (Romans 7:25, NLT)

Victory is not found in willpower. Victory is not found in self-help. Victory is not found in spiritual grit. Victory is found in a Person—Jesus Christ. Paul is brutally honest. Even knowing Jesus is the answer does not automatically make right choices easy. Judas stood closer to Jesus physically than nearly anyone in history, yet betrayed Him. Exposure to truth does not guarantee submission to truth. We do not drift into holiness. We choose obedience. We yield to the Spirit. We submit our minds, wills, and emotions to God.

Already, But Not Yet

Romans 7 must be read alongside Romans 8. There is a deliberate tension. Romans 7 shows struggle. Romans 8 declares freedom. Romans 7 feels heavy. Romans 8 breathes triumph. That is the Christian life—already free, not yet perfect. Already saved, not yet fully sanctified. Already belonging to Christ, still learning to think like Christ. Paul begins Romans 8 with the words every weary believer needs:

> "So now there is no condemnation for those who belong to Christ Jesus." (Romans 8:1, NLT)

No condemnation, even when you struggle. No condemnation, even when you fall.

No condemnation, even when your mind feels like a battlefield. Then he adds:

> "And because you belong to him, the power of the life-giving Spirit has freed you from the power of sin that leads to death." (Romans 8:2, NLT)

You belong to Jesus. Not to sin. Not to shame. Not to self. It is only when the mind settles there—on belonging to Christ—that the battle shifts. So how do we win? We fix our thinking on Christ. We do not let emotions outrank truth. We ground our minds in Scripture. We align desires with God's will. We cooperate with the Spirit. We refuse to accept slavery when freedom has been given. Your thoughts matter. Your inner world matters. Your mental life matters to God. Winning the war of the mind does not mean the battle disappears. It means the outcome is secured. It means temptation no longer reigns uncontested. It means sin no longer has automatic authority. It means when your heart stumbles, your renewed mind anchors you back to Christ.

Romans 7 does something precious for believers. It normalizes the struggle without normalizing sin. It admits the battle without surrendering. It confesses weakness while clinging to hope. It allows us to say, "Yes, I struggle. Yes, I fail. Yes, I wrestle with thoughts. But I am not abandoned. I am not condemned. I am not defeated. Christ is my answer."

Have you ever settled your soul on something good, and your mind refused to rest? Then Romans 7 is for you. How do you win the war in your mind? You settle it on Jesus. You return again and again to the truth that you belong—not to sin, not to fear, not to failure—but to Him. And when your mind is anchored in Christ, peace follows. Because in Him, even in the tension, the victory is already won.

Chapter 7 Reflection Questions
Winning the War with Your Mind

1. Why do believers still struggle with sin even after salvation?
2. What role does the mind play in spiritual obedience and holiness?
3. How can emotions mislead us if they are not anchored in truth?
4. Why is honesty about spiritual struggle important for the Christian life?
5. How does Romans 7 point us toward hope rather than despair?

CHAPTER 8

Does the Holy Spirit Live Within You?

Romans 8

If Romans 7 feels like a war inside the believer, Romans 8 sounds like victory. Many theologians call this one of the greatest chapters in the Bible, the "sparkling jewel" of Scripture. Paul has just confessed the inner tension believers experience—the pull of sin, the frustration of weakness, the mental war between desire and action. But the opening words of Romans 8 announce something breathtaking:

> "So now there is no condemnation for those who belong to Christ Jesus." (Romans 8:1, NLT)

No condemnation. No eternal guilt. No looming judgment. For the believer, condemnation is not delayed; it is canceled.

Romans 7 ends with agony: "Who will rescue me?" Romans 8 begins with assurance: *Jesus already has.* That is the hinge of Christian hope. What the law could not do, God did. What human strength could not accomplish, the Spirit accomplishes. Romans 8 is a chapter of confidence, clarity, comfort, and calling. It explains how believers truly live, not by religious rule-keeping but by the power of the Holy Spirit.

The Spirit Who Sets Us Free

Paul explains that the Spirit of God liberates us from the tyranny of sin. The law was good, but it could not change the human heart. It revealed sin. It exposed failure. It made guilt undeniable, but it could not free. Only the Spirit can do that. Paul declares,

> "The power of the life-giving Spirit has freed you from the power of sin that leads to death." (Romans 8:2, NLT)

Notice that language: power. Freedom. Life. These are not abstract ideas. They describe how believers truly live. The Spirit does not make us religious; He makes us alive. Christianity is not moral behavior modification. It is participating in the very life of God. And when the Holy Spirit moves in, everything changes, especially what we desire. As we mature physically, our tastes change. Things we loved as children no longer satisfy us. Spiritually, the same should happen. Paul writes,

> "Those who are dominated by the sinful nature think about sinful things, but those who are controlled by the Spirit think about things that please the Spirit." (Romans 8:5, NLT)

Growth in Christ means our appetites shift. Over time, believers desire what God desires. Our concerns change. Our conscience sharpens. Our allegiance deepens. The Holy Spirit is not a vague force. He is a Person within us producing new longings, new instincts, and new affections. Without Him, we cannot stand against sin. With Him, we are not powerless. We are equipped.

The Spirit Who Dwells in Us

Romans 8 insists on a truth we cannot overlook: the Holy Spirit lives in every true believer. Not near us. Not occasionally upon us. Within us. Paul puts it plainly:

> "You are controlled by the Spirit if you have the Spirit of God living in you. And remember that those who do not have the Spirit of Christ living in them do not belong to him at all." (Romans 8:9, NLT)

The Spirit is not optional. He is essential. He is the mark of belonging to Christ. His presence defines our identity. That is why what controls you is so important. Who shapes your thinking? Who forms your desires? Who guides your decisions? The Spirit's presence is not theoretical; it is experiential. Romans 8 tells us exactly how we can recognize His work.

The Spirit Who Leads

First, the Spirit leads believers. Paul writes:

> "For all who are led by the Spirit of God are children of God." (Romans 8:14, NLT)

Being led by the Spirit is not like being yanked by a leash or dragged against your will. It is not a chaotic emotional impulse. The Spirit's leading gives direction, confidence, and clarity rooted in God's truth. Being led by the Spirit does not mean God reveals every step of our lives, but it does mean He faithfully guides us into obedience, godliness, and truth. Believers are not abandoned to instinct or culture. God Himself shepherds us.

The Spirit Who Replaces Fear with Confidence

Paul continues:

> "So you have not received a spirit that makes you fearful slaves." (Romans 8:15a, NLT)

Before Christ, fear ruled. Fear of judgment. Fear of exposure. Fear of failure. Fear of rejection by God. But the Spirit replaces crippling fear with security and holy confidence. Not arrogance. Not self-assurance. A confidence grounded in the character and goodness of God. The Spirit assures believers that they belong, that they are safe in God's grace, and that nothing has the power to separate them from His love. Good confidence is trusting God. Bad confidence is trusting self. The Spirit gives the former and removes the latter.

The Spirit Who Brings Intimacy

Then Paul reaches one of the most tender truths in Romans 8:

> "Now we call him, 'Abba, Father.'" (Romans 8:15b, NLT)

"Abba" is not formal. It is affectionate. It is deeply personal. It is like a child calling out "Daddy," not because of obligation but because of closeness. The Spirit invites believers into intimacy with God. Christianity is not merely believing in God; it is knowing Him. We are not tolerated citizens in His kingdom. We are beloved children in His family. In the ancient world, if sons disappointed their father, he could adopt a servant to inherit his estate, giving full status and blessing to someone who was not biologically connected to the Father. Paul draws from that world to explain our salvation. We were once slaves to sin, but God has adopted us as sons and daughters. We are not hired servants. We are family.

The Spirit Who Gives Security

But what about doubt? What about those moments when believers wonder, "Am I truly saved? Do I really belong to God?" Paul answers with assurance:

> "For his Spirit joins with our spirit to affirm that we are God's children." (Romans 8:16, NLT)

It is a ministry of the Holy Spirit to secure us—to whisper assurance when doubt rises, to anchor confidence when emotion wavers, to testify that our salvation is real and secure in Christ. Our confidence rests not in emotional highs or flawless performance, but in the Spirit's confirmation of God's promise.

The Spirit Who Defines Our Identity

Paul continues,

> "And since we are his children, we are his heirs." (Romans 8:17, NLT)

We are not spiritually homeless. We belong. We are heirs: recipients of God's riches, His future promises, His eternal glory. The Spirit does not merely comfort us; He defines us. He names us. He secures our place in God's family. Our identity is not fragile. It is anchored in adoption, sealed by the Spirit. This identity changes how we pray. How we endure. How we live.

The Spirit Who Helps Us Pray

Romans 8 acknowledges that life is still painful. Creation groans in brokenness. The world aches for redemption. And believers groan too. We long for healing, justice, renewal, and eternal wholeness. Sometimes the weight of life makes prayer difficult. Sometimes pain buries words. Sometimes we do not even know what to pray. Paul gives one of the most comforting truths in Scripture:

> "And the Holy Spirit helps us in our weakness... the Holy Spirit prays for us with groanings that cannot be expressed in words." (Romans 8:26, NLT)

When you cannot articulate the prayer, the Spirit does. When you are too weary to form words, the Spirit intercedes. When your prayers are confused, misguided, selfish, or weak, the Spirit redirects them. When your prayers are only tears or silence, the Spirit speaks for you. He is emotionally invested in you. He is your Helper, your Intercessor, your Advocate before the Father. God is so good that He has placed His Spirit within you to strengthen even your worst prayers and empower your best ones.

The God Who Holds the Future

Romans 8 then moves into some of the most profound and debated theological realities: foreknowledge, election, and predestination. Paul writes that God knew in advance who would be saved and predestined believers to be conformed to the image of Christ. Those He calls, He justifies. Those He justifies, He glorifies. These truths speak to God's sovereignty, His eternal plan, and His unwavering commitment to redeem His people.

Christians have long debated the precise mechanics of how election and human responsibility interact. Scripture affirms both God's sovereign purpose and our responsibility to share and receive the gospel. Paul's emphasis here is not to spark an argument, but to anchor assurance. However God works out the mysteries of salvation, one thing is clear. He is in control, and His saving work is certain. There are things about God we will never fully grasp because He is God. As Deuteronomy 29:29 reminds us, some mysteries belong to Him alone. But what He has revealed, we are called to trust and obey.

The Spirit and the Goodness of God

Romans 8 famously declares,

> "And we know that God causes everything to work together for the good of those who love God." (Romans 8:28, NLT)

This does not mean everything *is* good. It means God sovereignly works good from everything. Suffering is real. Pain is real. But God is faithful. He redeems. He restores. He does not abandon His children. And that crescendo leads to one of the great climaxes of Scripture: If God is for us, who can be against us? Who can accuse those whom God has chosen? Who can condemn those God has justified? Nothing can separate us from His love. Not hardship. Not persecution. Not struggle. Not fear. Not even death. Paul closes with a thunderous declaration:

"Nothing in all creation will ever be able to separate us from the love of God."

(Romans 8:39, NLT)

That's right. Nothing.

Does the Holy Spirit Live Within You?

Romans 8 invites a deeply personal question: Does the Holy Spirit live in you? If you belong to Jesus, the answer is yes. And how do you know?

- The Spirit leads.
- The Spirit replaces fear with confidence.
- The Spirit creates intimacy with the Father.
- The Spirit secures assurance.
- The Spirit defines identity.
- The Spirit intercedes for you.
- The Spirit empowers living.

If you long to grow deeper, begin with prayer. Even small prayers work in big ways. You do not need eloquence. You need dependence. The Spirit meets you in weakness, not strength. He shapes your heart. He assures your soul. He renews your mind. He anchors you to Christ. Romans 8 declares a breathtaking truth: The Christian life is not lived alone. God Himself dwells within His people. He leads. He helps. He comforts. He secures. He loves. And because the Spirit lives in us, we live loved and unashamed.

Chapter 8 Reflection Questions
Does the Holy Spirit Live Within You?

1. What does "no condemnation" truly mean for the believer?
2. How does the Holy Spirit free us from the power of sin?
3. What does it mean to be led by the Spirit in everyday life?
4. How does the Spirit replace fear with confidence and assurance?
5. How does knowing the Spirit lives within us reshape how we live, suffer, and hope?

CHAPTER 9

God's Selection of Israel

Romans 9

Romans 9 begins not with an argument but with anguish. Paul opens this chapter—not by dissecting theology—but by revealing his broken heart. He writes with "unending grief" because so many of his fellow Jews have rejected Jesus as the Messiah. He even goes so far as to say he would be "cursed" if it meant they could be saved. This is not academic for him. It is sacrificial love. Paul is not detached from what he teaches. His theology bleeds. His doctrine is pastoral. His heart is burdened.

Why is Paul so desperate? Because Israel has been so deeply blessed. God chose them, recipients of covenants, witnesses of miracles, bearers of the Law, heirs of the promises, and from them came the Messiah Himself. Yet many had missed Him. Romans 9 addresses the question: *If Israel was chosen, then why are so many rejecting Jesus? And what does God's selection of Israel have to do with our salvation?* Paul's answer takes us to the heart of God's sovereignty and grace.

Chosen for a Purpose, Not Privilege

Paul reminds his readers that God chose Israel, but chose it for mission, not for guaranteed salvation. God selected Israel as the nation through whom salvation would be made available to everyone—Jew and Gentile alike. God chose them to *carry* the promise, not to *monopolize* it. Being physically descended from Abraham does not automatically make someone spiritually part of God's family. As Paul writes, "The children of the promise" are those who respond in faith to Christ.

This distinction matters deeply. Salvation has never been about ethnicity, heritage, tradition, or spiritual pedigree. It has always been about grace received by faith. You are not saved because of where you were born, your religious history, or your family's walk with God. Salvation is always personal. Always dependent on God's mercy. Always tied to Christ.

Jacob, Esau, and the Mystery of God's Choice

To prove that point, Paul takes us back to the story of Jacob and Esau. They were twins. They shared the same parents. They shared the same bloodline. And yet God chose Jacob to carry forward the covenant line. This was not because Jacob was more deserving. Jacob's name literally means "cheater." His story reads like moral chaos—deception, manipulation, family dysfunction, fear, exile, and shame. Yet God chose to work through him anyway. Jacob did not deserve grace, but God used him anyway. That is the gospel. Paul quotes God's declaration from Malachi:

> "I loved Jacob, but I rejected Esau." (Romans 9:13, NLT)

This is not personal animosity. It is not God emotionally favoring one brother and despising the other. It is covenantal language, not emotional language. One lineage would be chosen to carry the covenant promise toward Christ. The other would not. One line was accepted as the vessel through which redemption would come. One line was not. God was sovereignly working through history to bring salvation to the world. Jacob's story reminds us of something deeply hopeful: God works through deeply flawed people. If Jacob can be used, so can we. If grace can redeem him, it can redeem anyone.

Is God Unfair?

That question naturally arises: *Is God unjust? Is it unfair that He chose Jacob and not Esau? That He chose Israel and not another nation?* Paul's answer is direct: "No. God is God." He is sovereign. He does not owe grace to anyone. The miracle is not that God didn't choose everyone. The miracle is that He chose anyone. Paul makes it clear:

> "So it is God who decides to show mercy. We can neither choose it nor work for it."
> (Romans 9:16, NLT)

Salvation does not originate in our effort, intelligence, morality, achievement, religious zeal, or spiritual heritage. It rests on God's mercy. He saves because He is gracious. We receive because God is good.

Pharaoh, Hard Hearts, and God's Purpose

Then Paul moves from Israel's national history to a personal example: Pharaoh. Scripture states plainly: "God hardened Pharaoh's heart." But Scripture also repeatedly states: "Pharaoh hardened his own heart." Which one is it? It is both.

Pharaoh defiantly rejected God. He resisted the truth. He hardened himself in rebellion. And God allowed his hardened state to display His power. But there is something important to notice. Scripture gives no example of God hardening someone who sincerely seeks Him. God does not block the repentant. He does not deny the sincere. He does not turn away the humble. Hardening comes to those who defiantly resist grace.

Paul's point is profound: God is sovereign, but humans are responsible. God's purpose stands. Human decisions matter. Scripture consistently holds both truths without contradiction. Charles Spurgeon famously said when asked how he reconciled God's sovereignty and human choice: "I never reconcile two friends." They are not enemies. They are companions in God's mysterious redemptive plan.

Clay, the Potter, and the God Who Knows More Than We Do

Paul then asks the question we are all thinking: "Who are we to argue with God?" We are clay. He is the Potter. He sees the whole story. We see only fragments. God's sovereign purposes stretch beyond our comprehension. And yet Paul also says something astonishing: God is patient. God is merciful. God desires salvation. God delays judgment. Even those who persist in rebellion experience patience they do not deserve. God does not rush to condemn. He longs to save. Yet some will still reject Him.

The Bible does not flatten this tension. It preserves it. God is sovereign. People are responsible. We may never fully understand how these truths harmonize, but Scripture declares they do.

The Beauty Beyond the Debate

Romans 9 is often treated as a battleground. Paul intended it to be a blessing. He is not trying to stir controversy. He is revealing something beautiful—that God's purposes never fail. That His promises do not collapse. That He is faithful, powerful, sovereign, and good. God chose Israel not to exclude the world, but to bless the world. Jesus Himself is the fulfillment of Israel's calling. He is the true stairway between heaven and earth. Jacob dreamed of a ladder connecting man to God. Jesus declared Himself to *be* that connection. Through Christ, heaven opens to anyone who believes. That is why Romans 9 ends not with philosophical speculation but with an invitation.

So what do we do with a chapter like Romans 9? We do exactly what Paul does. We trust God's sovereignty. We rest in His goodness. We proclaim His salvation. We invite people to Jesus. Paul does not conclude by saying, "So do nothing." He concludes with urgency:

> "But anyone who trusts in him will never be disgraced." (Romans 9:33, NLT)

We are not called to solve every mystery. We are called to proclaim every mercy. God's sovereignty does not make evangelism unnecessary; it makes it meaningful. God uses our witness. He works through our obedience. He honors our faithfulness. He saves those who call on Him. And anyone may come. Every sinner, wanderer, skeptic, struggler, and prodigal. Every "Jacob." Every person who feels unworthy. Everyone is valuable to Jesus.

Romans 9 should not leave believers anxious. It should leave us at peace. Your salvation is not fragile. It is not hanging by a thread of your performance. It rests in the sovereign hands of God. Your past does not disqualify you. Your weakness does not surprise Him. Your future is secure because God is faithful. Jacob was deeply flawed. Yet God redeemed him, renamed him, and used him. He can do the same for you. Romans 9 is not ultimately about arguments. It is about assurance. God is sovereign. God keeps His promises. God brings salvation. God invites the world. God saves by grace. And Jesus is the way up to heaven.

Chapter 9 Reflection Questions
God's Selection of Israel

1. How does Romans 9 help us trust God's sovereignty even when we don't understand fully?
2. Why is God's mercy always undeserved and always gracious?
3. What does Israel's story teach us about God's faithfulness?
4. How should believers respond to the mystery and greatness of God's plans?
5. How does this chapter deepen humility and worship?

CHAPTER 10

WHO DOES GOD SAVE?

ROMANS 10

Romans 10 sits at a powerful intersection of theology and urgency. Paul is burdened for his people, passionate about the gospel, and deeply aware of how dangerously easy it is to miss God's plan by trying to create our own. Romans 9 magnifies God's sovereignty in salvation. Romans 10 emphasizes our response—what it means to believe, to confess, and to call on the name of the Lord.

I remember the day God saved me. Unfortunately, not the exact date (I should've written it down), but the moment is still vivid. I was seven years old at Hopewell Baptist Church in Louisville, Kentucky, where my dad was the pastor. I remember my thoughts as I walked the aisle during the invitation. *I'm not walking to my earthly father in this moment. I'm walking to my heavenly father.* That same year, we moved to St. Petersburg, Florida. Then, as an eight-year-old, I can still see myself sitting in our sunroom in the church parsonage, wrestling with the question: *Is it real? Is my salvation true?* And deep within me, the Holy Spirit settled it with a clear, steady answer: *Yes.* Even so, my spiritual journey didn't end there. In college, the questions came back in a different form. *Do I really believe all this? Or is it simply what I was raised to do?* God used those seasons, too, to press my faith from inherited to owned.

Paul opens the chapter with deep emotion: "Dear brothers and sisters, the longing of my heart and my prayer to God is for the people of Israel to be saved" (Romans 10:1, NLT). He loves Israel. He knows God loves Israel. And yet, Israel missed the heart of salvation. They had zeal, but it was misdirected zeal. They clung to their own way instead of trusting God's way. They believed effort, obedience to the law, and religious identity could save them. But Paul states plainly, "For Christ has already accomplished the purpose for which the law was given. As a result, all who believe in him are made right with God" (Romans 10:4, NLT). They thought the law would save them. They thought their effort and discipline would be enough. It never is.

Why Salvation Must Be Grace

Human effort can never accomplish the righteousness God requires. Even our best attempts fall short. God saves by grace because salvation must always point to His glory, not ours. It is relational, not transactional. The standard is perfection, and none of us is perfect. Even if God lowered the standard, we would still be left wondering whether we had done enough. Grace gives assurance. Grace gives peace. Grace gives certainty that salvation truly is a gift received by faith.

This is why Paul clarifies the simplicity and beauty of faith in Christ: "If you openly declare that Jesus is Lord and believe in your heart that God raised him from the dead, you will be saved" (Romans 10:9, NLT). Not "might be." Not "could be." Not "hopefully someday." Paul says you will be saved. That is the security of grace. That is the strength of the gospel. God does not invite us into uncertainty. He invites us into confident trust.

The Accessibility of Salvation

Romans 10 contains one of the clearest declarations of the accessibility of the gospel in all of Scripture. Paul says the gospel is not far away. You do not have to climb to heaven to find it. You do not have to dig deep into the earth to uncover it. Christ has already come. The gospel is near. Jesus is easily accessible and equally accessible to all.

Paul hammers home the wideness of God's invitation:

- "Anyone who trusts in Him will never be disgraced" (Romans 10:11, NLT).

- "There is no distinction between Jew and Gentile" (Romans 10:12, NLT).
- "Everyone who calls on the name of the Lord will be saved" (Romans 10:13, NLT).

Anyone. Everyone. No distinction. This was one of the greatest stumbling blocks for Israel. Many in Israel wanted a Messiah only for them. They longed for a Savior of Israel, not a Savior of the world. But Israel was never intended to be the end of God's mission. Israel was the means by which God's grace would extend to all nations. God declared through Isaiah, "I will make you a light to the Gentiles, and you will bring my salvation to the ends of the earth" (Isaiah 49:6, NLT). The people of God were never meant to hoard grace. They were designed to share it.

The church must hear that same warning today. We, too, can mistakenly believe God's work centers on us rather than flowing through us. We, too, can drift into comfort, identity, and self-focus. We must remember: we are not better than anyone else. The gospel breaks pride. The gospel humbles hearts. The gospel compels us outward.

God Calls Us to Move, Not Stand Still

Paul does not allow Romans 10 to remain theological theory. He makes it intensely practical. Salvation is available to everyone, but no one can respond unless they hear. And they cannot hear unless someone tells them. That reality underscores the urgency of the church. Paul writes,

> "How can they call on Him to save them unless they believe in Him? And how can they believe in Him if they have never heard about Him? And how can they hear about Him unless someone tells them?" (Romans 10:14, NLT).

God has entrusted the gospel to His people. Jesus sends His church. Believers proclaim. People hear. Hearers believe. Believers call. Those who call are saved. But if we never go, people never hear. If they never hear, they never believe. If they never believe, they never call. And if they never call, they are never saved.

This is why Paul declares, "How beautiful are the feet of messengers who bring good news!" (Romans 10:15, NLT). Feet are not naturally beautiful. But feet moving toward people in love, compassion, and mission are stunning in the sight of God. The Christian faith is just as much about using your feet as it is about using your mind. We are not called to be stationary disciples. A stationary Christian is a disobedient Christian. A stationary church is a disobedient church. The church is meant to move.

Using Our Feet: A Call to Our "One"

If salvation is accessible, if grace is for everyone, if the gospel saves all who believe, then what does obedience look like? It looks like movement. It looks like intentionality. It looks like love on mission.

One of the clearest applications is identifying and pursuing your "one." Your "one" is the person God has put in your life who does not yet know Christ or is far from Him. What do we do?

Pray for your one daily. Prayer itself glorifies God because praying for someone's salvation is an act of worship. Invite your one. Invite them to a worship service. Most people are far more open to an invitation than we believe. Be persistent, but positive. Do not give up. God does not give up on people. We should not either. Have you ever met anyone disappointed that Jesus saved them? Of course not. Every story of salvation is a story of grace, mercy, rescue, and new life. But those stories only happen when someone is willing to share. God's grace operates in partnership with God's people as they proclaim the gospel.

God's Heart and Our Calling

Romans 10 closes with a sobering image. God says of Israel, "All day long I opened my arms to them, but they were disobedient and rebellious" (Romans 10:21, NLT). It is a picture of God with open arms—longing to save, longing to restore, longing to redeem—while people resist, delay, and turn away. That picture should stir the church. God's arms are still open. The invitation still stands. Grace still saves. But the message must still be proclaimed. Romans 10 reminds us who God saves and how God saves. He saves by grace. He saves through faith. He saves without distinction. He saves anyone who calls upon the name of the Lord. And He sends His people so the world can hear.

God's grace is wonderfully simple: *No one deserves it. Anyone can receive it. But someone must share it.* So let us be loved. Let us be unashamed. Let us be a church with beautiful feet, moving toward the world, carrying the only news that truly saves.

Chapter 10 Reflection Questions
Who Does God Save?

1. What does it mean to confess and believe in Christ truly?
2. Why is faith in Jesus the only way of salvation?
3. Why must believers proclaim the gospel boldly and clearly?
4. What does this chapter teach about the urgency of evangelism?
5. How does Romans 10 challenge comfortable Christianity?

CHAPTER 11

The Mystery of God's Mercy

Romans 11

Every generation wrestles with mystery. Scientists explore the depths of creation. Philosophers probe meaning. Theologians examine divine truth. And yet, as Charles Darwin once confessed late in life, "The mystery of the beginning of all things is insoluble by us." For all his success, Darwin sadly admitted he could not fully resolve the deepest questions, and the wonder he once felt in nature began to fade. The universe is filled with mysteries far beyond our comprehension. Scripture recognizes this reality. But when it comes to salvation, God does not want to leave us in the dark.

Paul writes to the Romans, "I want you to understand this mystery" (Romans 11:25, NLT). In the biblical sense, a "mystery" is not something hidden forever; it is something once concealed that God has now revealed. What was partially known in the Old Testament—God's redemptive plan through the Messiah—is now fully unveiled through Jesus Christ. And in Romans 11, Paul unfolds one of the greatest mysteries of all: how God, in His sovereign mercy, is uniting Jew and Gentile into one redeemed people.

God Has Not Rejected Israel

Romans 11 opens with a crucial assurance: "God has not rejected His own people, whom He chose from the very beginning" (Romans 11:2, NLT). Though many within Israel rejected Christ, Paul wants believers to know God's covenant faithfulness remains intact. Israel's rejection is not total, and it is not final. Some did believe, but Paul grieves that many others developed hardened hearts. At the same time, through Israel's rejection, the gospel spread with power among the Gentiles. Paul even hopes Israel will see the faith of the Gentiles and be stirred with a holy jealousy that draws them back to Christ.

Paul puts it this way: "Now if the Gentiles were enriched because the people of Israel turned down God's offer of salvation, think how much greater a blessing the world will share when they finally accept it" (Romans 11:12, NLT). Here is the marvel of God's wisdom. He is working out redemption even through human rebellion. Paul is not interested in condemnation. He is pleading for restoration. Romans 11 is not a chapter of rejection. It is a chapter of hope.

The Olive Tree: A Picture of God's Family

Romans 11 is deeply anchored in the heart of God's mercy. Mercy and grace work together but are not identical. Mercy is God withholding the judgment we deserve. Grace is God giving us the salvation we do not deserve. Mercy rescues us from death; grace lifts us into new life. God's mercy is compassion in action, removing the penalty of sin. God's grace is abundant generosity that grants righteousness and adoption into His family. Across this chapter, Paul makes a stunning declaration: "God has imprisoned everyone in disobedience so He could have mercy on everyone" (Romans 11:32, NLT). Jew and Gentile alike are guilty. Jew and Gentile alike can be redeemed. That is the mystery Paul wants us to understand. God's mercy is far wider, deeper, and more powerful than human boundaries, failures, or categories.

To help us see this clearly, Paul uses the metaphor of an olive tree. Israel is pictured as the natural branches. Some were broken off because of unbelief. The Gentiles are pictured as wild branches, grafted into the tree by faith. This image communicates both inclusion and warning. Gentiles are graciously included in God's saving plan. But they must never become arrogant. God can just as easily graft Israel back in, and He intends to do so. God's mercy is expansive enough to restore Israel fully.

Paul describes it beautifully: "You, by nature, were a branch cut from a wild olive tree... if God was willing to do something contrary to nature by grafting you into His cultivated tree, He will be far more eager to graft the original branches back into the tree where they belong" (Romans 11:24, NLT). The message is unmistakable: God has not abandoned Israel. The story is not over. There is an anticipated future restoration, one that points toward the final uniting of Jew and Gentile in God's kingdom.

Paul goes on: "I want you to understand this mystery... Some of the people of Israel have hard hearts, but this will last only until the full number of Gentiles comes to Christ. And so all Israel will be saved" (Romans 11:25–26, NLT). This verse ties the church's present mission to God's future promises. God is not finished. His patience is purposeful. His mercy is unfolding.

God's Promise Secures Our Salvation

Romans 11 also reassures believers of God's commitment to His people. Salvation is not fragile. It is not unstable. It is grounded in God's covenant faithfulness. "For God's gifts and His call can never be withdrawn" (Romans 11:29, NLT). What God begins, He completes. What God seals, He keeps. God's seal of salvation is His eternal promise of protection and possession. Those whom God preserves will persevere. Saved people endure because salvation is secure in the faithful hands of God. That assurance allows believers to live without fear. We belong to God. We are His people. And the same God who grafted us in by grace can sustain us by grace until the end.

To bring the mystery of mercy down from the heights of theology into everyday experience, Romans 11 echoes the heart of Jesus' ministry. We see this beautifully illustrated in the story of Bartimaeus, the blind beggar in Mark 10. He sat on the roadside, marginalized, dismissed, and seen as cursed by many. When he learned Jesus was passing by, he cried out, "Son of David, have mercy on me!" The crowd tried to silence him, but he only cried louder. And then something remarkable happened: Jesus stopped. The King of the universe stopped for a desperate, broken man calling out for mercy.

Jesus restored his sight—but more than that, He saved him. And Bartimaeus followed Jesus. He likely followed Him to Jerusalem. To the cross. To the resurrection hope that changed everything. Bartimaeus' story is our story. Spiritually, we are all blind beggars in need of mercy. We have nothing to offer God but need. Yet when we cry out, He hears. He stops. He saves.

The Mystery Revealed

Romans 11 ends not with a debate, but with doxology. After unfolding this breathtaking picture of redemptive history, Paul can only worship: "Oh, how great are God's riches and wisdom and knowledge! How impossible it is for us to understand His decisions and His ways!" (Romans 11:33, NLT). The mystery remains beyond full comprehension, but not beyond faith. We cannot fathom the depths of God's mercy and grace, but we can know enough to receive it. This is the gift of Romans 11. God's mercy is wider than we imagine. His promises are stronger than our doubts. His plan is greater than our understanding. Jew and

Gentile. Past and future. Broken and restored. All of it converges in Jesus Christ, the One who rescues, the One who keeps covenant, the One whose mercy brings us home.

Romans 11 calls us to humility, gratitude, and hope. Humility, because salvation is entirely of mercy and grace. Gratitude, because we were once outsiders whom God graciously grafted in. Hope, because God is not finished. His mercy is still at work in the world, still reaching, still saving. The mystery of God's mercy has not been concealed from us. It has been revealed in Jesus Christ. We are invited not to solve it, but to trust it. Not to master it, but to marvel at it. And most importantly, to receive it.

Chapter 11 Reflection Questions
The Mystery of God's Mercy

1. How does Romans 11 reveal the depth of God's wisdom and mercy?
2. What does "grafted in" teach us about inclusion in God's family?
3. Why should God's mercy lead to humility instead of arrogance?
4. How does Israel's story encourage believers today?
5. How should this chapter move us toward worship rather than speculation?

CHAPTER 12

A Living Sacrifice to God

Romans 12

Romans 12 marks a decisive turning point in Paul's letter. After eleven chapters of rich doctrine, breathtaking grace, and a sweeping vision of God's saving work, Paul now shifts to the practical implications. Truth demands a response. Belief must lead to behavior. Paul is not content with Christians who merely understand theology; he calls us to embody it. Accepting Christian truth should lead to living a Christian life. So Paul begins with a plea: *"And so, dear brothers and sisters, I plead with you to give your bodies to God...Let them be a living and holy sacrifice."* The Christian life is worship—not confined to songs, Sunday services, or religious spaces—but expressed in the way we live, love, and serve every day. Worship, Paul reminds us, is not a spectator event. It is participation. It is engagement. It is offering ourselves fully to God.

A Paradox with Power: Living Sacrifice

The phrase "living sacrifice" sounds contradictory. Sacrifices die. They are placed on an altar and consumed. Yet Paul intentionally uses this paradox to capture what discipleship truly is. To be a living sacrifice means dying to self over and over again, surrendering the claim that our lives belong to us, relinquishing the right to live as we choose. It is the continual offering of body, time, desires, dreams, and direction to God.

But Paul's wording adds another profound layer. He writes to *brothers and sisters* (plural) about our *bodies* (plural), yet he calls us to offer a *sacrifice* (singular). It's not a grammatical mistake. Paul is writing to communicate an important theological reality.

> "And so, dear brothers and sisters, I plead with you to give your bodies to God because of all he has done for you. Let them be a living and holy sacrifice—the kind he will find acceptable. This is truly the way to worship him." (Romans 12:1, NLT)

The picture is corporate (plural). Christianity is not an individualistic (singular) spirituality. We are not scattered believers making separate offerings. Together we present one united sacrifice of obedience, faithfulness, and love to Christ. The church's surrendered life is a collective act of worship.

No One Sits the Bench

I played high school basketball. I know, you're wondering how on earth I didn't end up in the NBA. Just look at a picture of me, and you'll understand. But here's what I do know: I couldn't stand sitting on the bench. I was always thinking, ***Put me in the game, coach!*** And that's still true in life and ministry. If you're equipped and ready, you don't want to sit on the sidelines. You want to be in the game, where it matters.

Paul moves from worship to service because one naturally flows from the other. What we worship determines what we serve. God has not called His people to watch from the sidelines. Every believer has a role. Every believer is needed. In a healthy church, no one "sits the bench." Using his familiar body metaphor, Paul explains that just as a body has many parts with different functions, so does the church. Alone, no believer can accomplish God's mission. But together, as a unified body under Christ the Head, we can change the world. Membership in the church is not like joining a country club where you pay dues and receive services. It is joining a team, committing to a shared mission, engaging your gifts, and working together with coordinated purpose.

> "Just as our bodies have many parts and each part has a special function, so it is with Christ's body. We are many parts of one body, and we all belong to each other." (Romans 12:4-5, NLT)

The church is a place of belonging, honesty, and growth. It gives us community, a place to say, "This is where I belong." It provides accountability, space for honest evaluation of ourselves, especially against the temptation to think too highly or too lowly of ourselves. And it creates opportunity for spiritual growth as we discover and exercise God-given gifts.

Humility: The Posture of a Useful Church

Paul quickly confronts the greatest threat to a unified, serving church: pride. "Don't think you are better than you really are," he writes in Romans 12:3 (NLT). Pride places self at the center. Pride demands attention. Pride assumes that our importance exempts us from humility and service. But humility strips selfishness away. Humility recognizes that God owes us nothing and we owe Him everything. It acknowledges dependence on God rather than ourselves. It positions us not above others, but beside them, ready to serve. Paul insists that everyone must embrace this posture because spiritual gifts only become fruitful when powered by humility. A proud church is a spiritually stagnant church. A humble church becomes a useful church.

Paul also warns against false humility, the kind that constantly minimizes oneself to gain sympathy or attention. Whether we obsess over how great we are or how insignificant we are, both fixate on self rather than God. The gospel frees us from self-absorption, making us self-aware without being self-centered. We honestly evaluate who we are, how God has gifted us, and where we serve the body best.

Diversity: Strength, Not Threat

Alongside humility, Paul highlights diversity as essential to a healthy church. A church with many kinds of people—different backgrounds, ethnicities, ages, economic realities, and experiences—is a more gifted church. Diversity expands the capacity of the church to love, serve, and witness to the world. Unity is not sameness. It is many different people, shaped by many different stories, offering many different gifts, united under one Savior. In such a church, giftings are not rare bursts of extraordinary spiritual expression. Functioning in your gift is a normal part of the Christian life. Ordinary faithfulness, dependable service, flexible willingness, and consistent presence represent the everyday rhythms of a spiritually healthy congregation.

What a Living Sacrifice Looks Like

Paul refuses to keep his teaching in the realm of theory. Romans 12 paints one of the clearest portraits in Scripture of a life fully offered to God. When believers present themselves as living sacrifices, this is what begins to happen:

- They genuinely love rather than merely pretending.
- They honor one another above themselves.
- They reject laziness and pursue zeal in serving the Lord.
- They remain patient in hardship, joyful in hope, and persistent in prayer.
- They practice hospitality and generosity.

- They bless their persecutors rather than seek revenge.
- They celebrate with those who rejoice and grieve with those who weep.
- They pursue humility, avoid arrogance, and strive to live at peace with others.
- They refuse to be conquered by evil but conquer evil by doing good.

This is not sentimental kindness. It is love forged through sacrifice. It is steadfast goodness in a hostile world. Martin Luther King Jr. captured this spirit when he preached at Dexter Avenue Baptist Church in November 1957:

> "Hate is like eroding acid that eats away the best and the objective center of your life. So Jesus says love, because hate destroys the hater as well as the hated."

Love is not weakness. It is Christlike strength applied in the face of darkness.

Together for God's Mission

Romans 12 forces us to confront a critical question: What does it truly mean to follow Christ? According to Paul, it means daily surrender. It means humbly serving. It means joyfully embracing our place within the church. It means refusing to live for ourselves. It means not merely believing the gospel intellectually but allowing it to shape every thought, every decision, every relationship, and every habit.

When believers offer themselves to God, they become useful to Him. When churches embrace humility and diversity, they become powerful instruments of His grace. When congregations love sincerely, serve diligently, and refuse to repay evil with evil, they display the beauty of Christ to a watching world. Paul closes this chapter with a command that summarizes the entire Christian ethic.

> "Don't let evil conquer you, but conquer evil by doing good." (Romans 12:21, NLT)

This is not passive religion. It is active, resilient faithfulness. It is the church, united as one living sacrifice, joining God's mission in the world.

So what does it mean to be a living sacrifice? It means giving your life to God daily, humbly, and joyfully—together with others. It means choosing service over comfort, unity over isolation, and obedience over self-rule. It means stepping off the sidelines and into God's mission. It means being useful to Him. Romans 12 is not simply an instruction manual for Christian living. It is a vision, a picture of what happens when God's people truly believe the gospel and live it out together. It invites the church to be what Christ redeemed it to be: one body, deeply surrendered, boldly loving, and powerfully alive for God's glory.

Chapter 12 Reflection Questions
A Living Sacrifice to God

1. What does it truly mean to be a "living sacrifice"?
2. How does renewing the mind change the way believers live?
3. Why is humility essential to a healthy Christian community?
4. How do love, forgiveness, and service display gospel transformation?
5. Which part of Romans 12 challenges you most personally?

CHAPTER 13

The Christian Response to Government Authority

Romans 13

Romans 13 is one of the most practical and emotionally charged passages in Paul's letter. After calling believers to present their lives as living sacrifices (Romans 12) and to engage the world with humility, love, and sincerity, Paul addresses a difficult question: How should Christians respond to governing authorities? How should believers live under leaders, systems, and structures that are sometimes just and sometimes deeply flawed?

Paul begins with a commanding statement:

> "Everyone must submit to governing authorities. For all authority comes from God, and those in positions of authority have been placed there by God." (Romans 13:1, NLT)

Submission to government, Paul says, is part of our discipleship, because government itself is something God allows for the sake of human order. Governments are divinely given structures intended to serve society, restrain evil, and promote the common good.

The biblical worldview does not place government at the center of life, nor does it dismiss government as irrelevant. Instead, it recognizes that God is sovereign over all authority. Even when earthly rulers forget God, He has not forgotten His authority over them. When Jesus stood before Pilate, He reminded the Roman governor that he would have no power unless it were given from above. Earthly power operates within divine boundaries.

God's Intent for Government

When functioning as intended, government serves people and promotes the common good. Paul writes that rulers are meant to punish evil, protect citizens, maintain order, and allow people to live without fear. Obedience to civil law, paying taxes, and contributing to social responsibility are not merely civic duties; they are spiritual expressions of trust in God's design. Following the law and being a good citizen can be part of what it means to live with a "clear conscience" before God.

However, Scripture is clear that governments do not always operate as God intends. History has proven that earthly systems often drift from justice, morality, and accountability. Paul writes realistically, not naively. Romans 13 is not blind patriotism nor unthinking submission. It is sober recognition that government is intended to protect freedom, but it can also threaten it. So, when is resistance justified? When does submission to God mean refusing to submit to government?

The Limits of Obedience

The line is clear: when government commands what God forbids or forbids what God commands, believers must obey God rather than man. Peter and John, ordered to stop preaching about Jesus, refused and declared in Acts 4:20 (NLT), "We cannot stop telling about everything we have seen and heard." Civil disobedience is not about personal preference; it is about gospel loyalty. It is about preserving the mission of God above the control of government.

This is where religious liberty becomes essential. Religious liberty is not simply the right to gather on Sundays. It is the freedom to live out faith daily according to conscience. It is not a government-granted privilege; it is a God-given right. A government that protects freedom of belief serves all people well. A government that suppresses religious expression places itself in competition with God—and always loses. Yet, Scripture also gives us hope. If God can save any individual, He can revive any church. And if He can revive His church, He can restore a nation. God has turned rebellious civilizations back to Himself before. When nations forget God, He sometimes troubles them, not out of cruelty, but to turn them back to Him. If God is the problem for an unjust nation, then God must be the only solution for them.

Government, Kingdom, and the Heart of Allegiance

Paul understands something crucial: all earthly political systems are temporary. They rise, they fail, they change, and eventually they fall. But God's kingdom endures forever. Rome did not last. No empire has. No modern nation will. Christians honor government, but we do not worship government. We participate in society, but our highest allegiance belongs to Christ. What happens in our nation matters deeply, but our place in God's kingdom matters infinitely more.

Paul then shifts from government authority to personal responsibility. If the government is to function well, citizens must live rightly. Paul reminds believers that the law of God—summarized in the Ten Commandments and fulfilled in the Great Commandment—calls us to love.

> "Owe nothing to anyone—except for your obligation to love one another. If you love your neighbor, you will fulfill the requirements of God's law." (Romans 13: 8, NLT)

Love does not erase God's law. Love fulfills it. When we love God and love neighbor, we are already living out the heart of God's commands. Love restrains vengeance. Love rejects selfishness. Love compels integrity. Love keeps society humane and holy. Christian citizenship is not primarily about demanding rights; it is about demonstrating righteousness.

Urgency in a Broken World

Paul also injects urgency into the conversation. "Time is running out," he writes in Romans 13:11 (NLT). "The night is almost gone." The world is closer to judgment than it realizes. Eternity is nearer than we think. So believers cannot afford spiritual complacency. We belong to the day, not the night. We must "clothe ourselves with the presence of the Lord Jesus Christ" (Romans 13:14, NLT) and live visibly distinct lives in a dark world.

Yes, we should love our nation. Yes, we should honor those who serve in leadership. Yes, we should value unity amidst diversity and appreciate the beautiful vision of people from different backgrounds living together under shared ideals. But even that unity points beyond earthly identity to a greater reality—the kingdom of God, where people of every tribe, tongue, and nation worship the Lamb together. That future defines our present. So, how should Christians live?

- We respect authority but worship only Christ.
- We obey laws but remain faithful to God above all.
- We cherish freedom but use it to advance the gospel, not ourselves.
- We seek national well-being but prioritize eternal belonging.
- We participate in society, but we never forget that our ultimate citizenship is in heaven.

The government provides structure. God provides salvation. The government enacts laws for life. God transforms life. The government can protect freedom. God alone gives eternal freedom.

The Heavenly Kingdom Above Every Earthly Kingdom

Romans 13 asks us to hold tension: to live under earthly authority while living for heavenly authority. To love our country deeply without confusing it with God's kingdom. To advocate for righteousness without placing ultimate hope in politics. To obey faithfully yet be ready—if ever required—to courageously stand for Christ against any system that tries to silence Him. Ultimately, Paul leads us to a simple conclusion: the kingdom of God gives purpose now and forever. Our hope is not in elections, constitutions, or leaders, but in the reign of Christ. When believers grasp this truth, they become the most grounded citizens, the most peaceful participants, and the most hopeful people in any nation. Romans 13 does not call us to fear government. It calls us to honor God. It calls us to think biblically, live respectfully, love deeply, and anticipate confidently the unshakable kingdom that is already coming. So we submit, but wisely. We participate, but faithfully. We hope, but ultimately in Christ. Because when every earthly throne collapses, Jesus still reigns.

Chapter 13 Reflection Questions
The Christian Response to Government Authority

1. Why does Paul call believers to honor authority—even imperfect authority?
2. How can Christians live faithfully under governing systems?
3. How does love fulfill the law in public life?
4. What does it mean to "put on the Lord Jesus Christ"?
5. How does this chapter shape our witness in society?

CHAPTER 14

How to Contend for the Faith Without an Argumentative Spirit

Romans 14

I love a good fight. Not the dirty kind—more like a hockey game when the gloves come off, and it's a nice, clean scrap: a couple punches land, just a little bit of blood, and everybody moves on. There was nothing like watching Iron Mike Tyson in his prime, either. And then there's what might be the greatest fight in sports history: when 46-year-old Nolan Ryan put 26-year-old Robin Ventura in a headlock and absolutely pummeled him back in 1993. Now that I'm the old guy, I have even more respect for Ryan on that one.

Some people naturally love a good argument. Debate can be stimulating, sharpening, and even enjoyable when done in the right spirit. There is a place in the Christian life to "contend for the faith" and defend truth against false teaching. Scripture commands us to guard sound doctrine. But Romans 14 forces us to wrestle with an important question: *When does contending for truth turn into simply being argumentative?*

Paul is writing to a church filled with tension. Jewish believers, newly incorporated into predominantly Gentile congregations, carried with them deep convictions about diet and religious observance. Some believers still restricted their diets. Others ate freely. Some held tightly to traditional worship days. Others felt no obligation to those practices. These conflicts were not about core doctrine; they were about conscience. And conscience-driven disagreements can be some of the most emotionally charged.

Paul begins with a pastoral command in Romans 14:1 (NLT): "Accept other believers who are weak in faith, and don't argue with them about what they think is right or wrong." Strong believers—those more mature in understanding gospel freedom—were not to look down on newer or more cautious believers. Weak believers—those still clinging to old restrictions—were not to condemn those who did not share their scruples. Instead, believers were called to accept one another.

This is one of Scripture's clearest teachings on what theologians later called *adiaphora*: issues that do not ultimately matter in salvation or obedience to Christ. These are areas where Scripture leaves room for conscience, discernment, and spiritual growth. In such matters, the church is not meant to become a moral court handing down verdicts on every secondary issue. Instead, we hold to the fundamentals of the faith while extending grace on matters of preference and practice.

Weak and Strong: Not Labels of Worth

Paul calls those still tied to ritual "weak," not as an insult but as a description. Weak does not mean unfaithful; it simply means immature or still forming in understanding. Likewise, the "strong" are not superior Christians. They are simply believers who recognize that, in Christ, some external restrictions no longer apply. Those who are further along in maturity should help those who are still growing, not shame or pressure them. Romans 14 gives two main categories of tension:

1. How believers worship
2. What believers consume

Some argued over which day was best for worship. Others debated appropriate behavior on a worship day. Paul does not resolve the issue. Instead, he makes the deeper point: the timing of worship matters, but *the object of worship matters far more.* Whatever day believers choose, they must honor Christ. The early church worshiped at different times and in different settings. The emphasis is not on uniformity of schedule but faithfulness in gathering and devotion.

The other area of conflict was diet. Some believers abstained from meat out of conscience. Others enjoyed the freedom to eat. Paul affirms that in Christ all food is clean. Yet he also acknowledges that conscience matters. If someone believes something is wrong, forcing them to violate their conscience damages their spiritual health. Freedom should never be weaponized. Love always considers the impact of one's freedoms on another's faith. In both worship and diet, Paul's conclusion is the same: *these are not battles worth fighting*. Christians should not tear each other apart over matters Scripture leaves open. Keep the main thing the main thing. Avoid needless quarrels. Choose kindness over combativeness.

When Conviction Becomes Argumentative

Paul understands something deeply true about human relationships: sometimes we do not fight because we love truth; sometimes we fight because we love winning. There is a difference between conviction and combativeness. Conviction becomes toxic when it condemns others or when it becomes condescending. When disagreements turn into opportunities to elevate ourselves and belittle others, we have lost the heart of Christ. Scripture pushes back hard against a quarrelsome spirit. Believers should avoid slander. They should not constantly look for arguments. Instead, they should be eager to do what is good, gentle, and humble. Mature Christians do not look for fights. They look for opportunities to build up.

Romans 14 helps us develop a wise filter: *Does this issue really matter, or am I simply elevating my preference?* Some battles are worth fighting, especially when essential truth is at stake. False teachers should be confronted. Gospel distortion must be addressed. But when disagreements revolve around conscience issues, cultural differences, or personal practices, Paul urges restraint.

A Better Way: Honor Christ Above Argument

At the center of Romans 14 is a profound theological statement:

> "If we live, it's to honor the Lord. And if we die, it's to honor the Lord. So whether we live or die, we belong to the Lord." (Romans 14:8, NLT)

Our identity is not rooted in our opinions, our preferences, or even our convictions on secondary matters. Our identity is rooted in Christ. Our goal is not to win arguments; it is to honor Him. That shifts everything. If my words are designed merely to prove I am right, then I am serving my ego, not Jesus. If my "truth-telling" crushes someone who is weaker in faith, then I am acting in spiritual pride, not love. If exercising my freedom damages someone else's conscience, then I am acting selfishly, not sacrificially.

Paul urges believers to stop passing judgment and placing stumbling blocks in front of one another. Instead, he calls believers to aim for harmony and actively build one another up. It is far better to preserve unity than to win disputes. It is far more Christlike to lay down a freedom than to insist on it at another's expense.

Practical Wisdom for a Divided World

Romans 14 offers a remarkably timely word for today's culture, where outrage is rewarded, social media amplifies argument, and division is normalized. In such a world, the church is called to be different. Instead of seeking fights, believers should seek peace. Instead of inflaming tensions, they should speak words of encouragement. Instead of positioning themselves as moral referees over every disagreement, they should prioritize personal holiness before policing others. Paul gives practical guidance:

- Resist turning every disagreement into a battle.
- Shift focus from winning arguments to honoring Jesus.
- Ask whether your stance builds faith or creates stumbling blocks.
- Choose words that encourage rather than inflame.
- Do not weaponize knowledge, maturity, or theology.
- Use your spiritual strength to serve, not to dominate.

Sometimes the most mature thing a believer can do is say nothing. Sometimes the most loving thing a believer can do is quietly hold a conviction without demanding that others adopt it. Sometimes the most Christlike act is to step back from a debate for the sake of unity.

Belonging to the Lord Together

Romans 14 is ultimately about what kind of community the church will be. Will it be a battleground of egos or a family marked by grace? Will it be a place where believers feel constantly evaluated, or one where they are encouraged to grow? Will it be known more for arguments or for love? Paul calls the church to something better: a community where believers are patient with one another, gentle in disagreement, and focused on Christ above all. Because at the end of the day, what matters most is not our ability to debate, defend, or dismantle someone else's viewpoint. What matters most is that we belong to the Lord, together, and that our lives—and even our disagreements—reflect His love. Romans 14 reminds us that sometimes the most spiritual thing we can do is step away from the fight, lay down our pride, and build someone up instead. Because while a good debate may be enjoyable, a transformed life for Christ is far better.

Chapter 14 Reflection Questions
How to Contend for the Faith Without an Argumentative Spirit

1. Why do believers sometimes disagree, and how should we handle it?
2. What matters most when disputable issues arise within the church?
3. How does love guide Christian freedom?
4. Why must unity matter deeply to believers?
5. How can we honor Christ while differing in conscience?

CHAPTER 15

Living Right in a World Full of Wrong

Romans 15

Paul has spent most of his letter to the Romans explaining the gospel—why we need it, what Christ has done, how we are saved, and what new life in Christ looks like. But Romans never remains only theological. Truth leads to transformation. Belief shows up in behavior. Doctrine becomes discipleship. As Paul draws the letter toward its conclusion in Romans 15, he returns to the heartbeat he began with: believers are both loved and unashamed. We are "loved by God" (Romans 1:7, NLT) and therefore "unashamed of the gospel" because it is "the power of God at work" (Romans 1:16, NLT). That identity shapes how we live in a world full of spiritual confusion, relational tension, and moral wrong.

Romans 15 shows us how loved, unashamed people live. Paul writes to a church he has never visited, yet he commends them: they are "full of goodness" and "know these things well" (Romans 15:14, NLT). This is a mature church. But even healthy believers need reminders. Even strong Christians must be called forward. And even faithful churches must be encouraged to stay faithful. Paul is bold because even the strongest church never outgrows the need for intentional obedience.

A key theme of Romans 15 is unity within diversity. Throughout chapters 14 and 15, Paul addresses those he describes as "weak" and "strong" in faith. These are not insults or spiritual value statements. Rather, they describe believers at different stages of maturity. Some, mostly from Jewish backgrounds, still felt bound to certain rituals and traditions. Others, walking freely in their new identity in Christ, no longer felt such restrictions. The danger was pride on one side and judgment on the other. So Paul calls the church to a deeper kind of strength: the kind that serves.

> "We who are strong must be considerate of those who are sensitive about things like this. We must not just please ourselves." (Romans 15:1, NLT).

Christian strength is not independence. It is not self-assertion. It is not insisting on your way or proving you are right. Strength looks like sacrifice. Strength looks like patience. Strength looks like love. True spiritual maturity shows itself in humility and service, not dominance or preference.

This call to serve reflects the example of Christ Himself. Paul reminds us that even Jesus—the rightful King of the universe—did not come to be served but to serve and to give His life (Mark 10:45). Christ absorbed insult, carried our burden, and bore our sin. If the Son of God used His strength to serve, then His people must do the same. Serving others becomes one of the best ways to live right in a world full of wrong.

The Three-Part Strategy: Bear, Build, and Bless

Paul helps us think about this calling through a simple but profound three-part strategy: *bear, build, and bless.* First, believers are called to *bear the burdens of others.* The spiritually strong carry more weight, not less. Just as a physically stronger person has greater responsibility in a conflict to control their power, the spiritually mature bear greater responsibility in relationships, church life, and mission. Strength is not permission to push others around; it is the capacity to lift others up. When we bear with the weak, we are reflecting the heart of Christ, who bore the ultimate burden of our sin.

Second, Paul calls us to *build others up.* "We should help others do what is right and build them up in the Lord" (Romans 15:2, NLT). Encouragement is not optional in the Christian life. The church is not a gathering of critics but a community of builders. We build one another through prayer, truth, patience, presence, and grace. Paul ties this directly to Scripture when he writes,

"Such things were written in the Scriptures long ago to teach us. And the Scriptures give us hope and encouragement as we wait patiently for God's promises to be fulfilled" (Romans 15:4, NLT). When God's people live in God's Word, they become people of hope. When a church is deeply rooted in Scripture, it gains the patience, endurance, and encouragement needed to persevere in a broken world. The Bible is God's revelation of Himself to show us the way to hope.

This is why neglecting Scripture is so spiritually dangerous. Paul emphasizes that Scripture forms, strengthens, instructs, and sustains believers. To ignore the Word is to weaken the soul. To remain biblically disconnected is to drift toward discouragement and confusion. Satan does not have to destroy a believer; he only needs to distract them from the Word. But when we read, meditate, and submit to Scripture, hope is rekindled, endurance grows, and obedience strengthens. The Bible is inspired by God, is infallible in its truth, and is the final authority for believers. It does not simply inform us; it transforms us and anchors us in a hopeful future.

Third, Paul calls the church to *bless the neighbors around you.* Because the Roman believers were "full of goodness," that goodness was meant to overflow. Holiness is never meant to remain internal, private, or contained. The goodness God places in His people is designed to spill outward into neighborhoods, workplaces, friendships, and nations. The church is not only a spiritual family but also a sent people. Paul speaks of his passion to preach the gospel where it has not yet been heard, while also affirming the faithful work of established churches where the gospel is already present. Every church carries a dual calling: local ministry and global mission. We serve "here" while also sending "there." This is the true meaning of *ekklesia* (the Greek word for "church"): God's called-out people, gathered for Christ and sent for Christ.

The Gospel for All People

Romans 15 also emphasizes unity in the gospel for all people. Jew and Gentile alike share in the promises of God. Paul quotes multiple Old Testament passages to demonstrate that God always intended salvation to extend to the nations. Christ is the fulfillment of that promise. This unity is not created by human effort but by Jesus Himself. When believers trust Him fully, they find joy, peace, hope, and unity through the power of the Holy Spirit (Romans 15:13). Division fades when Christ becomes greater. Conflict loses power when worship grows stronger. The more our hearts magnify Jesus, the less room there is for pride, bitterness, or self-centeredness.

Romans 15 closes with a glimpse of Paul's pastoral heart. He celebrates what God is doing, shares his mission plans, asks for prayer, and expresses love for the church. Paul is both theologian and shepherd, missionary and pastor, thinker and servant. His life models the balance he calls the church to embody: bold gospel conviction with gentle gospel compassion—truth spoken in love. Conviction expressed through service—a strong prophetic voice guided by a gentle shepherd's hand.

So how do believers live right in a world full of wrong? Romans 15 gives a clear and compelling answer. We serve others rather than ourselves. We bear with the weak instead of judging them. We build others instead of tearing them down. We bless neighbors instead of ignoring them. We root ourselves in Scripture instead of drifting with culture. And above all, we love Jesus deeply, trusting Him completely, and living unashamed of His gospel. When God's people live this way, something powerful happens. Hope grows. Unity strengthens. Witness expands. And the church shines brightly in a dark world. Loved by God and unashamed of the gospel, we can live faithfully, courageously, and joyfully until every promise of God is fulfilled.

Chapter 15 Reflection Questions
Living Right in a World Full of Wrong

1. What does it mean to bear with the weak instead of judging them?
2. How does Scripture anchor us when culture shifts?
3. Why must believers be committed both to local faithfulness and global mission?
4. How does unity display the power of the gospel?
5. How can your church live "loved and unashamed" in today's world?

CHAPTER 16

The Secret Revealed

Romans 16

Romans 16 may seem, at first glance, like a list of names and final thoughts. But this concluding chapter is anything but an afterthought. Paul closes his grand theological masterpiece with warmth, warning, mission, praise, and ultimate hope. In Romans 1, he began with identity—believers are "loved by God" and called to be His people; therefore, they are unashamed of the gospel. Now, in Romans 16, he shows what loved and unashamed people do. They live on mission. They protect what matters. They endure spiritual battle. And they lift a doxology of praise because the "secret" of salvation has been revealed in Christ.

Paul begins by commending Phoebe, the likely carrier of this precious letter to Rome. Faithful believers risked much simply to ensure God's Word reached God's people. Then he greets many co-laborers. This is the longest greeting section in any of Paul's letters. These names are not filler; they represent faithful friends, courageous servants, and spiritual family members who lived the gospel. They remind us that ministry is always relational and that the advance of the kingdom happens through people who are willing to work, sacrifice, risk, and persevere. Priscilla and Aquila "risked their lives" for Paul. Phoebe put herself in danger. Others were imprisoned. Many "worked hard" for the gospel. The chapter testifies that the mission of Christ is not for the casual; it is for the committed. We are not called to comfort. We are called to mission.

Paul then shifts to a warning. The church must not only proclaim truth but also protect truth. "Watch out," he writes in Romans 16:17, for those who cause division and deceive innocent people. The church has a dual responsibility in a dangerous world: ensure safety within and confront danger without. The gathered church must be a place where the vulnerable are protected, disciples are nurtured, and people experience spiritual safety. At the same time, the church must send people out into spiritually dangerous and difficult places with courage, conviction, and faith. A safe church produces courageous Christians. This balance is essential. A fearful church never sends. A reckless church never protects. A faithful church guards truth, protects people, and boldly enters the world with the gospel.

This missional calling flows from the great "secret" revealed in Romans 16:25–26. What was once hidden in part has now been fully revealed in Christ. In the Old Testament, believers trusted forward. They looked toward a Messiah whose name and timing they did not yet know. They lived in faithful anticipation. Now, through Jesus, the mystery is unveiled, the plan is complete, and salvation is fully revealed to all who believe. What was once a "mystery" is no longer. The gospel has gone public. God does not hide salvation; He declares it. Redemption is not available for one group but for Jew and Gentile alike. The plan of God is global, eternal, and unstoppable.

This revealed mystery is why Paul erupts into doxology. A doxology is an expression of praise—a declaration of glory to God. The word comes from two Greek ideas: ***doxa*** (glory, worthiness) and ***logos*** (word, speech). Because God is worthy, we give Him glory. Because salvation has been revealed, we worship. Twice, Paul declares, "All glory to God." This is the right response to the gospel. Doctrine leads to devotion. Theology leads to worship. The unveiling of God's redemptive plan does not merely inform the mind; it ignites praise in the heart.

Yet Romans 16 also reminds us that this revealed secret demands action. Only the church has been given the mandate to share this Good News. The task has not been assigned to governments, universities, the entertainment industry, media, or businesses. The responsibility belongs uniquely to the people of God. From the beginning of the letter, Paul declared that believers are loved by God and unashamed of the gospel. Now, at the conclusion, he reinforces that calling. The mission is worth the risk. The gospel is worth our lives. The church exists to proclaim Christ until every nation hears.

Romans 16 also reminds believers of something deeply encouraging and deeply needed in a broken world: Satan is already defeated. Paul writes in Romans 16:20, "The God of peace will soon crush Satan under your feet." This takes us back to Genesis 3:15—the first announcement of the gospel. After humanity's fall, God promised the serpent's head would one day be crushed. Satan would wound, but Christ would conquer. On the cross, Jesus delivered that fatal blow. The enemy remains active, but not victorious. He fights from defeat. His power is limited. His strategy is deception because he lacks ultimate authority. The forces of darkness are real, but the power of light is greater. Christ has overcome, and believers share in His victory.

This means believers do not live in fear. We do not cower in anxiety. We do not shrink back from mission. We recognize spiritual warfare is real, but we also know Satan's authority is broken. His heel strikes still hurt, but his head is crushed. Christ reigns. Light always overpowers darkness. Jesus Himself declared that Satan has no power over Him. Therefore, those who belong to Christ live in confidence, courage, and assurance. We walk into dangerous places with steady faith, knowing that Jesus is with us and His victory is ours.

Romans began with good news of identity and calling. It ends with the same truth ringing loudly. We are loved by God. We are unashamed of the gospel. The mystery has been revealed. Salvation has come. The church must proclaim it boldly. We protect the vulnerable, courageously face danger, refuse deception, and live in victory because Christ has already conquered. The gospel is not merely a message to admire; it is a mission to carry. What was hidden is now declared. The story that began before creation is fulfilled in Christ and continues through His people until the whole world hears.

Paul's final word is fitting: not fear, not anxiety, not uncertainty, but praise.

> "All glory to the only wise God, through Jesus Christ, forever. Amen." (Romans 16:27, NLT)

Romans 16 ends where every redeemed life will ultimately lead: eternal worship of a glorious God. The secret is revealed. The Savior reigns. And the church carries His name to the world.

Chapter 16 Reflection Questions
The Secret Revealed

1. What do the many names in Romans 16 teach us about ministry and mission?
2. Why is gospel work always relational and costly?
3. Why must the church both protect truth and proclaim truth?
4. How does the revealed "mystery" of salvation lead us to worship?
5. What does it mean to live unashamed of the gospel until the mission is complete?

CONCLUSION

Loved by God, Unashamed of the Gospel

Romans is not merely a letter. It is not simply a theological treatise or a collection of doctrinal arguments. Romans is the Spirit-breathed foundation of Christian identity, security, calling, and mission. From its sweeping explanation of the human problem to its breathtaking announcement of God's solution, from justification to sanctification, from Israel's story to the church's mission, Romans grounds believers in the gospel so deeply that they can live confidently, courageously, and joyfully in any age.

Paul began this letter by rooting believers in identity: "You are loved by God." That declaration frames everything else. Before the church is called to obey, proclaim, serve, or suffer, it is first called to rest in the unshakable truth that believers are deeply and eternally loved by God. That love is not abstract. It is not sentimental. It is not tentative. It is demonstrated, proven, and embodied at the cross and secured forever through the resurrection of Jesus Christ. The gospel does not simply offer help. It brings life. It does not simply advise moral improvement. It rescues, redeems, restores, reconciles, and renews.

And because believers are loved, they live unashamed. "I am not ashamed of the gospel," Paul declares. Romans explains why. The gospel is not weak. It is power. It is not a suggestion. It is salvation. It is not limited to certain people. It is for all who believe. The gospel answers humanity's deepest questions: Who are we? What is wrong with the world? Can anyone be saved? What must we do to be right with God? What hope do we have in life and death? Romans refuses shallow answers. It refuses to flatter human pride or diminish human sin. It confronts our depravity and proclaims God's mercy. It declares that righteousness does not come by human effort, moral achievement, heritage, law, ritual, or religious association. Righteousness comes by grace alone, through faith alone, in Christ alone.

Romans takes us into the courtroom, where all the world stands guilty. Then, just as the verdict settles in, heaven speaks again—and the guilty are declared righteous through Jesus Christ. Justification changes everything. We are forgiven. We are accepted. We are reconciled. We have peace with God. No condemnation remains. No wrath lingers. In Christ, believers stand secure, not because of their goodness, but because of His grace.

But Romans does not end with justification. The same grace that saves also transforms. Romans teaches us that sin's penalty is removed, but it also proclaims that sin's power is broken. Through union with Christ, believers are no longer slaves to sin. The Holy Spirit lives within them, reshaping desire, renewing the mind, forming holiness, strengthening endurance, and producing obedience. Romans is honest that the struggle remains. The battle for the mind is real. The tension between flesh and Spirit is ongoing. But the presence of struggle does not mean the absence of hope. The Spirit assures believers that they belong to Christ, empowering them to live with confidence rather than fear, assurance rather than anxiety, and freedom rather than bondage.

Romans also lifts our eyes beyond ourselves. It pulls us into the grand story of redemption—Israel's calling, God's faithfulness, His sovereign mercy, His unfolding purposes throughout history, and His commitment to bring salvation to the nations. The gospel is bigger than any individual life. It is bigger than any one people group. God is writing a global, eternal story of redemption. Jew and Gentile alike are grafted into His redemptive plan. His mercy is wider than we imagine, deeper than we deserve, and stronger than human resistance.

Romans then turns from what God has done to what God calls His people to do. Doctrine moves to devotion. Belief moves to behavior. Theology produces transformation. Those who have received mercy become living sacrifices. Those who have been justified by grace are called to live in grace-shaped community. Romans paints a portrait of gospel-formed people: humble, loving, unified, generous, gracious, honoring authority rightly, resisting vengeance, pursuing peace, bearing with the weak, strengthening the church, and engaging the world with conviction and compassion.

Romans ends where it began, with love, identity, calling, and mission. It reminds us that the gospel advances through real people with real names, real sacrifices, and real obedience. The kingdom does not move forward through spectators but through servants. Not through the casual but through the committed. The church must proclaim truth and protect truth. It must nurture believers and send believers. It must be both safe and bold—guarding the flock while courageously entering a dangerous world with a dangerous message of transforming grace. A fearful church will never send. A reckless church will never protect. A faithful church will do both.

Romans also ends in worship. After unfolding the mystery of redemption—once hidden, now revealed—Paul erupts in praise. That is the right response to the gospel. If Romans only informs our minds but does not ignite our worship, we have not truly understood it. Doctrine should not make believers colder. It should set hearts ablaze. Theology should not produce arrogance. It should produce awe. Romans shows us a God who is sovereign yet merciful, holy yet gracious, just yet saving, transcendent yet near. No wonder Paul declares, "All glory to God!" The only right way to end Romans is on our knees in gratitude and praise.

So what does Romans leave us with?

- Romans leaves us grounded. In a shifting world, believers have an unchanging gospel. Our assurance is not rooted in feelings, circumstances, or performance but in God's finished work in Christ.

- Romans leaves us humbled. There is no room for boasting, pride, superiority, or self-righteousness. We are not saved because we are good. We are saved because God is gracious.
- Romans leaves us secure. No condemnation remains. No accusation stands. No power can separate believers from the love of God in Christ Jesus our Lord.
- Romans leaves us transformed. We do not return to the old life. We do not continue as slaves to sin. By the Spirit, we pursue holiness, renewal, obedience, and Christlikeness.
- Romans leaves us unified. The gospel destroys barriers. Jew and Gentile, strong and weak, differing backgrounds and cultures—all are one in Christ.
- Romans leaves us sent. The gospel is too glorious, too necessary, too powerful to keep to ourselves. We are called to proclaim it, defend it, live it, and take it to the ends of the earth.
- Romans leaves us worshiping. After all the truth declared, warnings given, hope proclaimed, and calling announced, we end where Paul ends, lifting our hearts in doxology. The gospel is not merely something to understand. It is something to adore.

And ultimately, Romans leaves us living as its great theme declares: loved by God and unashamed of the gospel. Loved, not temporarily, conditionally, or partially, but eternally. Unashamed, not tentative, embarrassed, or hesitant, but bold, joyful, and confident. Loved by God. Unashamed of Christ.

Grounded in the gospel. Empowered by the Spirit. Sent into the world. Anchored in hope until every promise of God is fulfilled. That is the story Romans tells. That is the identity it gives. That is the calling it lays upon the church. And that is the invitation it extends to every believer—to live loved, to live unashamed, and to live fully for the glory of God.

Other books by Sam Rainer:

The Goodness of God in the Chaos of Our World

Make My Church Safe

The Surprising Return of the Neighborhood Church

Understanding the Bible as a Whole

Church Revitalization Checklist

7 Basics of Belonging

Leading Change When Nobody Wants It

Obstacles in the Established Church

Essential Church

www.ingramcontent.com/pod-product-compliance
Lightning Source LLC
LaVergne TN
LVHW010948110826
845149LV00015B/3261

* 9 7 9 8 9 9 5 4 0 3 4 0 1 *